OXFORD MEDICAL PUBLICATIONS

Miscarriage

THE FACTS

Miscarriage

THE FACTS

GILLIAN C. L. LACHELIN

Senior Lecturer in Obstetrics and Gynaecology
University College London

Oxford   New York   Tokyo
OXFORD UNIVERSITY PRESS
1985

Oxford University Press, Walton Street, Oxford OX2 6DP

Oxford New York Toronto
Delhi Bombay Calcutta Madras Karachi
Kuala Lumpur Singapore Hong Kong Tokyo
Nairobi Dar es Salaam Cape Town
Melbourne Auckland

and associated companies in
Beirut Berlin Ibadan Nicosia

Oxford is a trade mark of Oxford University Press

Published in the United States
by Oxford University Press, New York

British Library Cataloguing in Publication Data
Lachelin, Gillian C. L.
Miscarriage: the facts.—(Oxford medical publications)
1. Miscarriage
I. Title
618.3'92   RG648
ISBN 0-19-261472-X

Printed in Great Britain by
Richard Clay (The Chaucer Press) Ltd.
Bungay, Suffolk

Preface

Miscarriages are unfortunately very common. Approximately one in four women who become pregnant will have one or more miscarriages. They usually cause considerable distress to the potential parents, who are likely to experience a number of emotions including profound disappointment, fear of the process of miscarriage and about the future, sadness, self-pity, anger, grief, guilt, feelings of inadequacy, failure, and helplessness, and sometimes prolonged depression.

It is natural to seek an explanation for the miscarriage and to wonder whether it was precipitated by a particular action. In fact, in the majority of cases the pregnancy was never viable because of a fault very early in development. From the point of view of the individual, reproduction is not a very efficient process in either the plant or animal kingdoms and this is true for human reproduction as well. This is not very surprising when we consider that every one of us started life as a single cell, formed by fusion of a cell from each of our parents, and that our bodies are eventually made up of millions and millions of highly specialized cells formed by repeated division of this first cell. A very small fault in cell division at an early stage can lead to failure in the normal development of the embryo or placenta and hence to a miscarriage. It is really much more surprising, when we think about it, that any of us come through this process at all than that some pregnancies end in miscarriage.

In many instances the specific cause of a particular miscarriage will never be known. In a few cases a cause can be found. The potential parents should derive comfort from the fact that there was no bar to conception in their case and that their problem is not one of infertility. Statistically the likelihood of a successful pregnancy is good even after two or more miscarriages.

The aim of this book is to try to give an understanding of the

Preface

events of early pregnancy and the factors that may adversely affect the development of the embryo. The process and causes of miscarriage are discussed, and advice is given about future pregnancies. It is hoped that when a miscarriage does occur the people involved will be able to cope better if they have some understanding of what is happening.

G.C.L.L.

London
February 1985

Contents

I

Definition of the terms 'miscarriage' and 'abortion'

Many people are unaware how frequently miscarriages occur and how much distress they may cause to the couples concerned. Probably between 15 and 20 per cent, or more, of confirmed pregnancies end in miscarriage. This means that well over 100 000 pregnancies end in miscarriages that are recognizable as such in Britain each year, and that several hundred such miscarriages occur each day. It is likely that the true rate of early pregnancy loss is in fact much higher than this—possibly more than 75 per cent of human conceptions are lost—but many of these losses occur before the women concerned are aware that they are pregnant, i.e. before a menstrual period is missed (see Chapter 6).

To the outsider a miscarriage may appear as a bit of bad luck soon to be got over, but to the couple involved the loss of the pregnancy, even at a very early stage, may be utterly devastating and the miscarriage may have profound and prolonged emotional effects on them (see Chapter 10). Greater understanding of the reasons why miscarriages occur and of the process of miscarriage by the couple, and greater awareness of their needs and feelings by those with whom they come into contact, may help to alleviate the couple's distress to some extent.

The terms miscarriage and abortion are currently used interchangeably by doctors to mean the loss of a pregnancy from the uterus (womb) before 28 weeks' gestation. The phrases 'weeks' gestation' and 'weeks of pregnancy' are used to mean the number of weeks since the first day of the woman's last menstrual period, assuming that she has a roughly 28-day menstrual cycle, as the actual date of conception is not usually known. Thus 28 weeks of pregnancy (or gestation) means 26 weeks from conception, as ovulation usually occurs on about day 14 of a 28-day cycle.

The above definition of miscarriage and abortion is really no longer appropriate as more and more babies born before 28 weeks of pregnancy are surviving and developing normally. Babies born at 26 weeks' gestation have a better than 30 per cent chance of survival in a modern neonatal intensive care unit. It is likely that the terms miscarriage and abortion will be redefined in due course as the current definition is now clearly inappropriate, but, as it is the one in use at the moment and as most of the discussion in this book is related to early pregnancy loss, no attempt has been made to redefine the terms.

Many people find the interchangeable use of the words miscarriage and abortion upsetting as they feel that abortion implies deliberate termination of a pregnancy, but as the terms are used interchangeably in practice they have been used in this way throughout the book with appropriate adjectives where necessary to make the meaning clear.

Threatened miscarriage/abortion means that the woman experiences vaginal bleeding during the first 28 weeks of pregnancy. The bleeding may be slight or heavy and may or may not be accompanied by lower abdominal discomfort and backache. It is a relatively common situation and is discussed further in Chapter 4.

Spontaneous miscarriage/abortion indicates that the abortion occurred naturally and that it was not induced.

Complete abortion means that all the products of conception—the fetus (developing baby), placenta (afterbirth), and amniotic sac (membranes)—have been expelled from the uterus, and that the uterus is empty and a curettage (scrape) is not necessary. Very early miscarriages, before 7 weeks' gestation, are usually complete.

Incomplete abortion implies that only some of the products of conception have been expelled and that some remain in the uterus. This means that there is a risk of further bleeding and of infection, and that curettage is required.

Missed abortion indicates that the fetus has died but that a miscarriage has not yet occurred.

2

Septic abortion means that the abortion is accompanied by infection of the cavity of the uterus.

The last four conditions are discussed further in Chapter 5.

Recurrent miscarriage/abortion is a term usually used to mean that a woman has had three or more consecutive miscarriages; it is discussed further in Chapter 9.

2

Ovulation, conception, and early development of the embryo

The female reproductive organs consist of the ovaries, Fallopian tubes, uterus (womb), cervix (neck of the womb), and vagina (front passage) as shown in Fig. 2.1.

In a woman of reproductive age the ovaries are almond shaped and are each approximately 3 cm × 1.5 cm × 1 cm in size; they are whitish in colour. They each contain several thousands of ovarian follicles, which were formed when the woman herself was a fetus. Each follicle consists of an immature ovum (egg) surrounded by layers of smaller cells.

The Fallopian tubes are pink and are each approximately 10 cm long. The part of the tube nearest the uterus is very narrow (less than 1 mm internal diameter) whereas that part—known as the ampulla—which is furthest from the uterus is wider. It is in the

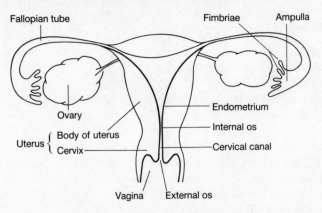

FIG. 2.1. The female reproductive organs.

4

ampulla that fertilization normally takes place. The outer end of each tube is formed of several tentacle-like processes, known as fimbriae, which help the ovum to enter the tube at the time of ovulation.

The uterus varies in size from one woman to another. In a woman of reproductive age who has not borne children it is usually approximately 8 cm long, 5 cm wide at its widest point, and 3 cm from front to back. It has a thick muscular wall. The upper part of the uterus is known as the body of the uterus; its outside is smooth and pinkish in colour whereas the inside is lined with tissue known as the endometrium, most of which is shed with each menstrual period. The body of the uterus is usually tilted forwards (anteverted), but in about 15 per cent of women it is tilted backwards (retroverted). This is usually of no importance and does not make miscarriage more likely.

The lower part of the uterus is known as the cervix. It protrudes into the top of the vagina, and can be felt by inserting a finger into the vagina. Its vaginal surface is normally covered with smooth pink tissue. The inner area of the junction of the body of the uterus and the cervix is known as the internal os. The opening from the lower end of the cervical canal into the vagina is called the external os.

Ovulation

The processes of ovulation and menstruation are controlled by a complicated interplay between the pituitary gland and the ovaries (Fig. 2.2).

The pituitary gland is only about 1 cm in diameter but it is a very important structure indeed. It lies near the middle of the skull under the lower surface of the brain. It exerts control over several organs (including the thyroid gland, the adrenal glands, the ovaries, and the testes) by producing various hormones. Hormones are chemical messengers produced in one part of the body which affect the function of cells in other parts of the body. The pituitary hormones that affect the function of the ovaries are known as follicle-stimulating hormone (FSH) and luteinizing hormone (LH).

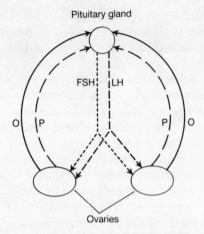

Pituitary gland

FSH LH

O P   P O

Ovaries

FIG. 2.2. The interplay of hormones between the pituitary gland and the ovaries: FSH, follicle-stimulating hormone; LH, luteinizing hormone; O, oestrogen; P, progesterone.

The average menstrual cycle is approximately 28 days in length. It begins on the first day of a menstrual period and lasts until the next period. The first half of the cycle is known as the follicular phase and the second half of the cycle (after ovulation) is known as the luteal phase (Fig. 2.3). The luteal phase usually lasts from 10 to 14 days. The follicular phase is more variable in length; it lasts about 14 days in an average cycle but is much longer in women with long cycles. Thus in a woman with a 35-day cycle the follicular phase lasts approximately 21 days.

During the follicular phase several of the many follicles present in the ovaries increase in size under the influence of the follicle-stimulating hormone produced by the pituitary gland. One follicle usually develops faster than the others and becomes the dominant follicle. As the follicles develop they secrete increasing amounts of oestrogen (one of the two sorts of female hormone) which cause regrowth of the endometrial lining of the uterus. The increasing oestrogen levels also affect the production and secretion of hormones by the pituitary gland and lead to a greatly increased release of luteinizing hormone on about day 13 of a normal cycle. This causes ovulation to occur approximately 24 hours later from the

6

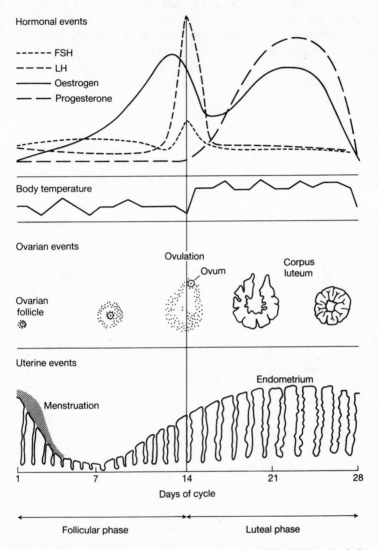

FIG. 2.3. The events of the normal menstrual cycle: FSH, follicle-stimulating hormone; LH, luteinizing hormone.

then fully developed dominant follicle (or occasionally from more than one follicle).

The fimbriae of the Fallopian tube become closely applied to the ovary during ovulation, and the ovum and its surrounding cells are drawn into and along the tube by the action of millions of cilia (hair-like processes) on the cells lining the tube and by the contractions of the tube.

Following ovulation the ovarian follicle develops into a corpus luteum (yellow body—so called because of its yellowish colour) (Fig. 2.3). The corpus luteum secretes increasing amounts of progesterone (the other female hormone) and also continues to produce oestrogens. Under the influence of progesterone there is further development of the endometrium in the luteal phase in preparation for the arrival of a fertilized ovum. If implantation (embedding) of an ovum does not ensue, oestrogen and progesterone levels fall, the endometrium disintegrates, and a menstrual period occurs with loss of blood and endometrial tissue (Fig. 2.3). If implantation does occur the corpus luteum continues to secrete increasing amounts of oestrogen and progesterone during the early weeks of pregnancy. The rise in progesterone levels in the luteal phase is responsible for the slight rise in body temperature (approximately 0.5 °F or 0.3 °C) that occurs after ovulation (Fig. 2.3). Measurement of the body temperature (first thing in the morning) during two or three cycles is helpful in showing whether a progesterone-producing corpus luteum has formed, and thus whether ovulation has presumably occurred. However, it is not a useful way of timing intercourse to coincide with ovulation in a particular cycle as the temperature rise may not be clear cut, and by the time that it is certain that the temperature has risen it may be too late for fertilization to take place.

Sperm production

Sperms are produced in large numbers in the testes and are stored in the male reproductive tract prior to ejaculation. Each ejaculate contains several million sperms. These are deposited high in the vagina during intercourse. Many of them rapidly penetrate the cervical mucus which is receptive to them around the time of ovulation, although not at other times in the cycle. They then pass into the uterus and along the Fallopian tubes which some of them reach within minutes of ejaculation. Their numbers decline markedly within 24 hours of intercourse, but a few may remain in the tubes and retain their fertility for more than 48 hours.

Fertilization

Fertilization of an ovum by a sperm normally takes place in the ampulla of one of the tubes; it is only possible for a few hours after ovulation. It is a highly complex process which has become better understood in recent years. It is at this time that many fetal chromosomal abnormalities arise; others arise during the earlier development of either the ovum or the sperm.

Chromosomes

Normal human cells contain 46 chromosomes comprising 22 pairs of non-sex chromosomes and one pair of sex chromosomes (Plate 1). In a female both the sex chromosomes are so-called X chromosomes; in a male there is one X chromosome and one Y chromosome in each cell. The chromosomes are made up of thousands of genes which transmit all the information necessary to allow development into a human being with characteristics (such as height, hair colour, blood group etc.) inherited from both parents.

In order to study the chromosomes of an individual, cells of the tissue to be studied—usually white blood cells from a blood sample in an adult or child, and amniotic fluid (the fluid surrounding the fetus) or placental, or fetal tissue in early pregnancy—are cultured in a specialized laboratory. A detailed study of the chromosomes can then be made.

At the time of fertilization each ovum or sperm contains half the number of chromosomes that are present in other cells, so that when they fuse the fertilized ovum will have the normal complement of 46 chromosomes. Thus each ovum has 22 non-sex chromosomes and an X chromosome, and each sperm has 22 non-sex chromo-

9

somes and either an X or a Y chromosome. If the fertilizing sperm bears an X chromosome, the fertilized ovum and all the cells into which it divides will contain two X chromosomes and the fetus will develop as a female. If the fertilizing sperm bears a Y chromosome, the fetus will develop as a male.

The process of production of the correct number of chromosomes in ova and sperms is very complex. It involves not just a simple halving of the chromosomes by one member of each pair of chromosomes being incorporated into each ovum or sperm, but an exchange of chromosomal material between the members of each pair of chromosomes before half the parental chromosomal material is incorporated into the new ovum or sperm. This allows great variety in the chromosomal make up of each individual ovum and sperm, and hence of each individual human being.

The process of integration of the chromosomal material of the ovum and the sperm at the time of fertilization is also highly complicated.

It is not surprising, therefore, that errors in the chromosomal make up of the fertilized ovum commonly occur. It is likely that they arise in well over 10 per cent of conceptions. In the great majority of these cases the chromosomal abnormality is incompatible with survival and the embryo dies during the early weeks of pregnancy. It has been found that a chromosomal abnormality is present in more than 50 per cent of confirmed pregnancies which end in miscarriage (see Chapter 7).

Implantation

The fertilized ovum begins to divide as it moves along the Fallopian tube. Its movement is caused by the beating of the cilia and by the muscular contractions of the tube. It probably enters the uterus after it has divided into 8 or 16 cells, about 3 days after fertilization. Cell division continues before the ovum implants in the suitably prepared endometrium about 6 or 7 days after fertilization, at which stage it is still smaller than a pin head.

The process of implantation is very complex, and not surprisingly many fertilized ova fail to implant satisfactorily and are lost at this time. Soon after implantation increasing amounts of a hormone known as human chorionic gonadotrophin (HCG) are made by the cells of the chorionic villi (early placental tissue) of the developing embryo. Low levels of this hormone can now be measured in blood and urine by sophisticated research methods, and so-called 'subclinical' pregnancies can thus be detected before a menstrual period has been missed, i.e. less than 14 days after fertilization. From studies involving such measurements of HCG in women trying to conceive it appears that between 10 and 30 per cent of embryos are lost during the second week after fertilization, without the women concerned being aware that they had been pregnant (see Chapter 6).

Further growth of the embryo

Following successful implantation further rapid growth and development of the embryo takes place. The embryo is very vulnerable to the effects of noxious agents such as certain infections (e.g. rubella (German measles)) and some drugs as the various organs develop. This is why it is important that women should have their immunity to rubella confirmed before they become pregnant, and why X-ray examinations and most drugs should be avoided when conception is a possibility.

3

Antenatal care in early pregnancy

In the majority of women no major complications occur in the first few months of pregnancy. None the less, serious problems can arise and it is very important that every woman should be seen early on, or preferably before she becomes pregnant if she has any medical problems, by the doctors who are going to look after her during her pregnancy. In Britain most women have their babies in hospital and the care of pregnant women is usually shared by the woman's general practitioner (or another general practitioner if her own general practitioner does not undertake antenatal care) and the doctors at the hospital where the baby is going to be born. In the United States, too, most babies are born in hospital. Prenatal care may be undertaken by a private doctor, or by a team of doctors at the hospital.

In Britain a woman should see her own general practitioner first and discuss the arrangements for her care during pregnancy with him or her. If the pregnancy has not already been confirmed it may be helpful to take an early morning urine specimen to the doctor's surgery at that time. The specimen should consist of a sample of urine passed first thing that morning into a clean jar. The equivalent of half a cupful of urine is enough—the rest can be discarded. The doctor can then arrange for a pregnancy test to be performed on the sample if necessary. Sometimes the test can be done immediately; sometimes the sample has to be sent away to be tested.

First hospital visit

Ideally the woman should be seen at the hospital for her first (booking) visit between 8 and 12 weeks after her last period, if she has not had any problems in this or any other pregnancy. If she has had problems it may be advisable for her to be seen sooner.

The purpose of the booking visit is literally to book a bed for the delivery and the postnatal period, as each hospital can only accommodate a certain number of patients, to check that the woman is healthy and that the pregnancy is proceeding normally, and to arrange for various blood tests and other investigations to be performed.

Routines vary from one hospital to another, but in general the woman will be asked a lot of questions about her past medical history and her previous obstetric and gynaecological history, and she will then be asked about the present pregnancy.

The urine will be tested for the presence or absence of protein and sugar and for evidence of infection. Routine blood tests will be arranged. The purpose of these is to establish the woman's blood group and to see whether she has any abnormal antibodies (such as Rhesus antibodies which could affect the baby), to make sure that she is not anaemic, and to determine whether or not she is immune to rubella (German measles) as a rubella infection in early pregnancy can have very serious consequences for the fetus. A blood test to exclude syphilis is also performed routinely in most hospitals, as this infection is so dangerous for the fetus (and the mother) and so easy to treat if it is diagnosed in time. Other tests, such as that for spina bifida, may be offered. These tests are discussed more fully later in this chapter.

At this visit or one arranged for a few days later she will be examined by one of the doctors. A general examination will be performed first. This will include measurement of her weight and blood pressure, checking for any signs of ill health, and an examination of her breasts and abdomen. A vaginal (internal) examination will usually be performed after this.

Some women are unhappy about having a vaginal examination, but it can give a considerable amount of important information that will help in the safe care of the pregnancy and there is no evidence at all that it can harm the pregnancy. It is essential that the woman has an empty bladder and that she is as relaxed as possible. Sometimes the examination is performed with her lying on her back and sometimes with her lying on her side. In either case the knees are drawn up. The doctor will usually first insert a smooth metal instrument (a speculum) into the vagina in order to look at the cervix (neck of the womb). A cervical smear is often taken at this time if one has not been done recently. If there are signs of infection or if the woman complains of excessive discharge, itching, or soreness a swab may be taken for culture. The doctor will then perform an internal examination with two fingers of one hand inserted into the vagina and with the other hand on the lower abdomen, so that the uterus can be gently felt between the fingers of the two hands. The purpose of this examination is firstly to confirm that the uterus is enlarged to the expected size, and secondly to check that there is no abnormality in the reproductive organs such as uterine fibroids, an ovarian cyst, or an ectopic pregnancy (a pregnancy in one of the Fallopian tubes). A preliminary assessment of the size of the birth canal is also made at this time.

Ultrasound

If there is any difference between the size of the uterus on examination and the size that the uterus is expected to be from the date of the last menstrual period, an ultrasound scan will usually be arranged (Plate 2). In some hospitals this is now performed routinely, but not all hospitals are able to offer routine scans to all antenatal patients although there are some advantages in being able to do so. For example, one of the most important things that a doctor needs to know about a pregnant woman is how far pregnant she is. This knowledge becomes vital if any problems arise or if the pregnancy becomes 'overdue'. It is easy to establish the duration of pregnancy fairly accurately in early pregnancy, but it becomes more difficult as pregnancy advances because different fetuses grow at different rates.

An ultrasound scan performed after 8 weeks' gestation will also show whether the fetus is alive or not as by this stage the heart can usually be seen to be beating. Evidence that the fetus is alive is obviously very reassuring to a woman who has previously had a miscarriage. Once the fetal heart can be seen to be beating the chance of a miscarriage falls to less than 5 per cent. It will prove that in this pregnancy at least a live fetus is present at this stage, and should the woman still be unfortunate enough to miscarry it will help her and her doctor to understand more about the type of miscarriage that she had. Follow up scans may be performed at intervals of 2-4 weeks and will show whether or not the fetus is continuing to grow satisfactorily.

Hormone levels

A great deal of work has been done on the measurement of hormone levels in early pregnancy. A hormone is a chemical messenger that is made in one part of the body and affects the functions of cells in various parts of the body. Some hormones, such as human chorionic gonadotrophin (HCG), which is made by the placenta and which forms the basis for the pregnancy test on an early morning urine sample, are almost unique to pregnancy; others such as progesterone and oestrogens are made in increasing amounts during pregnancy. Many attempts have been made to predict whether or not pregnancies will miscarry by measuring hormone levels in the first 3 months of pregnancy. So far no such measurements have been found to be infallible. Hormone levels are therefore not measured routinely in early pregnancy.

Blood test for spina bifida

In some hospitals all pregnant women are offered the opportunity of having the level of alpha fetoprotein (AFP) in their blood measured as a screening test for fetal spina bifida and other neural tube (spinal cord and brain) defects. In other hospitals the test is only offered to women who have already had a fetus with a neural tube defect or who have a family history of such a problem. If the fetus has a neural tube defect the level of AFP in the mother's blood will usually be higher than normal between 16 and 18 weeks' gestation. Unfortunately this test does not always give a clear-cut answer as, for example, the mother's dates may be wrong, there may be a fault in the laboratory measurement, or the level may be raised for a reason other than a fetal neural tube defect (such as a twin pregnancy or bleeding earlier in pregnancy) or for no obvious reason. If the level is found to be raised a repeat measurement will be arranged and an ultrasound scan will be performed to check the dates, to exclude twins, and to look at the fetus with particular reference to the spine and the head to make sure that they are developing normally. A few women will then be offered an amniocentesis (see below) so that the AFP level in the amniotic fluid can be measured, as this will give a more accurate prediction of fetal abnormality than measurement of the AFP level in the blood.

When discussing with a woman whether she would like to have her blood AFP level measured, it should be made very clear to her that just because a raised level is found on one test this does not necessarily mean that there is anything wrong with the fetus, otherwise she will understandably be even more anxious than necessary if someone telephones her and asks her to come for a repeat measurement and for a scan. Only in a small number of women who are recalled for a further test will there actually be a serious problem with the fetus.

Amniocentesis

Amniocentesis is the name given to the investigation that is performed when a sample of the amniotic fluid around the baby is taken for analysis, usually at about 16 weeks' gestation. A pool of fluid is located using an ultrasound scanner and a small area of the mother's abdominal wall is numbed with local anaesthetic. Amniotic fluid is then aspirated via a fine needle inserted through the numb area.

The test carries a small risk of miscarriage (about 0.5 per cent). It is therefore only performed in special circumstances such as the detection of a fetal chromosomal or biochemical abnormality in a pregnancy particularly at risk for such as abnormality, if the mother would want a termination of pregnancy if a serious abnormality were to be detected.

Later in pregnancy amniocentesis can be used to determine the severity of Rhesus disease in a woman with Rhesus antibodies (see p. 52).

Fetoscopy

In this investigation a thin lighted telescope is introduced into the amniotic sac through the mother's abdominal wall under local anaesthesia at about 18 weeks' gestation in order to look at either the fetus or the fetal blood vessels. A sample of fetal blood or even fetal tissue can be obtained for analysis in order to detect certain fetal abnormalities in appropriate cases. This investigation carries a greater risk of causing miscarriage than amniocentesis (about 3 per cent) and is therefore only used in exceptional circumstances.

Chorionic villus sampling

This is a new technique in which a small sample of chorionic villi (early placental tissue) is obtained at about 9–10 weeks' gestation via the cervical canal under sterile conditions. It can be used to diagnose certain very serious hereditary blood disorders (e.g. thalassaemia major) and metabolic diseases (e.g. Tay Sachs disease) when there is a very high risk of these occurring in the fetus.

The advantage of the technique is that it can be performed in the first 3 months of pregnancy, allowing simple vaginal suction termination to be performed when this is felt to be the right course of action. The disadvantage is that currently it carries a risk of miscarriage in up to 5 per cent of cases. It is therefore only used at the present time when there is a very high risk (25 per cent or more) of a very serious inherited condition. If, as is likely, the risk of miscarriage can be reduced with improved techniques, chorionic villus sampling will become a preferable alternative to amniocentesis in many cases—for example in the diagnosis of fetal chromosomal abnormalities such as Down's syndrome.

Do's and don'ts in early pregnancy

Diet and drugs

It is advisable to have a well-balanced diet, to stop smoking, and to reduce alcohol consumption before conception occurs. No unnecessary drugs should be taken by a woman who is trying to conceive. If drugs are needed for the treatment of a medical disorder it is very important for the woman to discuss these with her general practitioner or with the hospital doctor who is looking after her, so that changes can be made if necessary before conception.

Exercise

There is no evidence that moderate exercise does any harm in early pregnancy and women can safely continue their usual forms of activity unless these are very strenuous or dangerous or any complications of pregnancy arise. Thus there is no reason why pregnant women should not continue with such activities as walking, swimming, and playing tennis. Undue exhaustion should, however, be avoided.

Sexual intercourse

This is very unlikely to cause any harm to the pregnancy unless there has been any bleeding. It may, however, be best for a woman who has had several miscarriages to abstain from intercourse in early pregnancy.

Announcing the pregnancy

It may be wise not to tell too many people too soon about the pregnancy in case a miscarriage does occur—it can make the miscarriage even more distressing if too many people know about the pregnancy. On the other hand support from close friends would be very important if a miscarriage were to occur, and therefore there is no reason why they should not know about the pregnancy from an early stage.

4

Threatened miscarriage and ectopic pregnancy

Vaginal bleeding in early pregnancy is a very common problem. It may come from inside the uterus and be due to a complication of pregnancy such as a threatened or actual miscarriage, or an ectopic pregnancy (pregnancy in one of the Fallopian tubes), or it may come from the cervix. In many cases the bleeding is slight and settles down and its source is never identified with certainty. Bleeding in early pregnancy is maternal in origin—it does not come from the fetus.

Threatened miscarriage

The main symptom of a threatened miscarriage is vaginal bleeding which is due to some degree of separation of the placenta or membranes from the wall of the uterus. The bleeding is usually red to start with and then changes to brown as the amount of loss diminishes. There may be some lower abdominal discomfort and backache, similar to that felt with a period. Usually the loss stops after a few hours or days and the pregnancy continues normally. In some cases, however, the fetus will die, or it may have already died before the bleeding started, and a miscarriage will eventually take place.

If the bleeding becomes heavy with clots or if the pain becomes severe it is likely that a miscarriage is occurring and the general practitioner should be contacted. Any tissue that is passed should be kept so that it can be looked at by the doctor and if necessary sent for examination under a microscope.

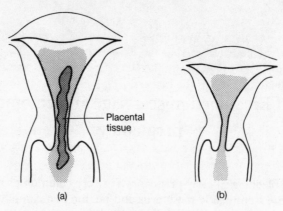

FIG. 4.1. (*a*) Incomplete abortion; (*b*) complete abortion.

Possibility of ectopic pregnancy

If the abdominal pain is very severe or unrelenting the possibility of an ectopic pregnancy must be considered. This is a potentially very dangerous condition as internal bleeding occurs and this can lead to collapse and even to death if an emergency operation is not performed in time (see p. 23).

Diagnosis of threatened miscarriage

The doctor may perform an internal examination in order to distinguish between a threatened and an actual miscarriage. With a threatened miscarriage the uterus is the appropriate size for the length of gestation and the cervical canal is 'closed' (i.e. its normal diameter). If a miscarriage has already occurred the products of conception (placental tissue and the amniotic sac, which may or may not contain a fetus) may have been only partially expelled. They may be lying partly in the uterus and partly in the cervical canal which will be open (incomplete abortion). If the products of conception have been completely expelled the uterus will have become smaller and the cervical canal will have become 'closed' again (Fig. 4.1).

If a diagnosis of threatened abortion is made an ultrasound scan will probably be arranged in due course to confirm that the fetus is alive and to exclude the unlikely possibility of a hydatidiform mole (see Chapter 7). If it is not possible for this to be done a pregnancy test may be performed, but this can remain positive even after the fetus has died as the placenta may continue to make human chorionic gonadotrophin (HCG) and it takes some days for HCG to be cleared from the body.

Treatment of threatened miscarriage

It is very difficult to prove that any particular measure reduces the likelihood of a threatened miscarriage proceeding to a miscarriage. In most cases the pregnancy will continue normally without any special action being taken; in other cases the fetus will already have died and nothing can possibly save it.

The two general measures which seem most likely to be beneficial for a precarious pregnancy, and which are most often recommended, are resting and refraining from sexual intercourse.

Rest is interpreted by different people in different ways. In general if the abdominal discomfort and bleeding are slight then it may not be important for the woman to retire to bed. If, however, there is fairly heavy bleeding bed rest may lessen the amount of bleeding and it may also reduce the chance of miscarriage. It is hard to prove that it helps, but it is possible that it makes all the difference in a few cases if the fetus is still alive.

The rationale behind avoiding sexual intercourse is that the uterus contracts during orgasm, and if the pregnancy is already in danger of being expelled the contractions may be sufficient to precipitate a miscarriage. Another danger of intercourse is the possibility that infection may be introduced into the uterus if a miscarriage has already begun.

Drug and hormone treatment of threatened miscarriage

A large number of remedies have been tried but there is no evidence that any drugs or hormones have any beneficial effects at all and indeed some of them actually have short-term, or more often long-term, ill effects.

Short-term ill effects include prolonging the time to spontaneous miscarriage when the fetus has already died. This may occur with some progestogens (progesterone and progesterone-like drugs).

The main long-term worry with drugs and hormones is that they may adversely affect the fetus. This effect may be apparent when the baby is born—thus thalidomide caused severe limb deformities, and some progestogens used in the past caused masculinization of some female fetuses—or it may not be apparent for many years—thus in the last few years it has been found that the daughters of women who were given stilboestrol (a synthetic oestrogen) in pregnancy sometimes have an abnormally developed uterus and are also at risk for developing a rare type of vaginal cancer in their teens and early twenties. Stilboestrol is no longer given to pregnant women.

Sedatives. Sympathetic explanation and reassurance are preferable to the administration of sedatives which cannot help to save the pregnancy and which may even be harmful.

Analgesics (pain-relieving drugs). Pain is not usually a prominent feature of a threatened miscarriage, and if pain is continuous or severe the woman should be seen by her doctor. It is likely that a miscarriage is occurring or, much less commonly, that the pregnancy is in one of the Fallopian tubes (ectopic pregnancy) instead of in the uterus (see p. 23).

Hormones. There is no definite evidence that any miscarriages are due to inadequate production of any particular hormone. Low hormone levels may sometimes be found prior to miscarriage, but this is usually because the pregnancy has already failed; the low levels are not usually the cause of the failure.

Hormones that are still occasionally used in an attempt to support an early pregnancy include HCG, progesterone, and non-masculinizing progestogens. There is no evidence that any of these are effective although it is possible that they may be in a very few cases. If the fetus is alive there is a more than 90 per cent chance of the pregnancy continuing without any treatment following a threatened abortion. Hormonal treatment, which may cause problems, is therefore hardly ever justified.

Outlook for the pregnancy following a threatened abortion
The outlook for the pregnancy following a threatened abortion is very good if the fetus is still alive. Thus in more than 90 per cent

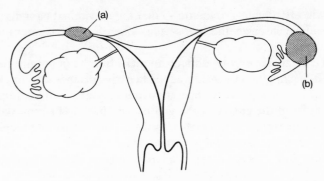

FIG. 4.2. Two common sites for an ectopic pregnancy: (*a*) in the narrow part of the Fallopian tube; (*b*) in the wider part of the Fallopian tube.

of such cases the pregnancy will end with the birth of a live healthy baby. Many women are anxious that there may be an increased risk of their baby being abnormal when they have had bleeding in early pregnancy, but fortunately this is not so. There is, however, a slightly increased risk of premature labour and of impaired placental function later in pregnancy, and it is therefore important that the pregnancy should be carefully monitored with these problems in mind.

Ectopic pregnancy

Ectopic means out of place, and the term ectopic pregnancy is used to describe a pregnancy that has implanted outside the uterine cavity. This occurs in about 1 in 200 pregnancies in this country. The most common site for an ectopic pregnancy is in one of the Fallopian tubes. As the pregnancy develops the tube stretches and may rupture (Fig. 4.2).

If the pregnancy implants in the narrow part of the tube rupture of the tube and internal haemorrhage leading to severe abdominal pain, faintness, and collapse are likely to occur very early in the pregnancy—sometimes before the woman has realised that she is pregnant. More commonly the pregnancy implants in the wider part of the tube—the ampulla—and internal bleeding then occurs a little later in the first trimester (first three months of pregnancy) and will often be less dramatic so that the abdominal pain may be less sudden in onset and less severe. There may be some vaginal bleeding.

The diagnosis may be difficult to make but the important thing is that it should be considered. When the diagnosis is obvious an emergency abdominal operation under general anaesthesia is required and the affected tube will usually have to be removed as it will be so damaged. A blood transfusion may be needed to replace the blood lost into the abdominal cavity.

If the diagnosis is uncertain a laparoscopy will often be recommended. In this procedure (which is usually done under general anaesthesia) a lighted telescope (laparoscope) is inserted just under the umbilicus, after inflating the abdominal cavity with carbon dioxide, and a good view of the uterus, tubes, and ovaries can be obtained. If the diagnosis of ectopic pregnancy is confirmed the gynaecologist will proceed straightaway with an abdominal operation to remove the affected tube.

Other causes of bleeding in early pregnancy

Bleeding in early pregnancy may be due to complications of pregnancy as described above or it may be due to other causes such as a cervical erosion, a cervical polyp, or very rarely cancer of the cervix.

Cervical erosion

This rather inappropriate term is used to describe a change in the cervix which commonly occurs during pregnancy and at other times of hormonal change (such as when a woman is taking a hormonal contraceptive pill). The cervical canal is normally lined by mucus-producing cells which make it look red and rough to the naked eye, whereas the vaginal surface of the cervix—the ectocervix—normally appears pink and smooth (Fig. 4.3). With the alteration in hormone levels that occurs in pregnancy the red mucus-producing tissue lining the cervical canal grows out onto the ectocervix and it too becomes red and rough. This appearance is known as a cervical erosion, although the cervix is not in fact eroded (Fig. 4.3).

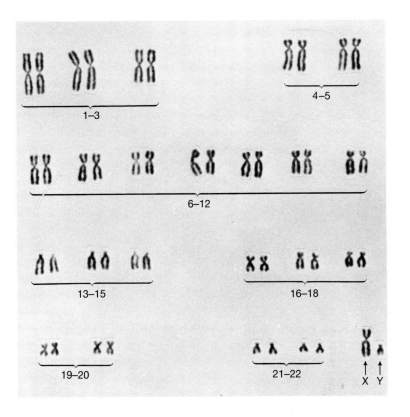

PLATE I. The 23 pairs of chromosomes of a normal male.

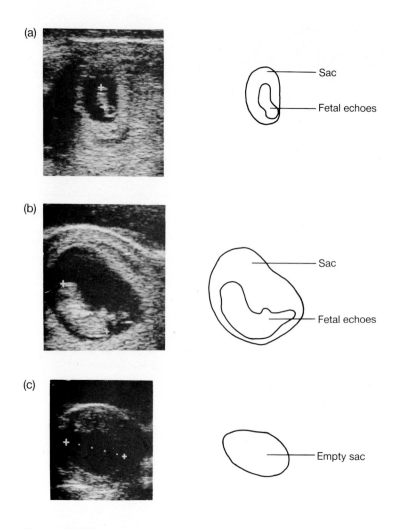

PLATE 2. (*a*) Ultrasound scan at 7 weeks' gestation showing normal fetal echoes. (*b*) Ultrasound scan at 10 weeks' gestation showing normal fetal echoes. (*c*) Ultrasound scan showing empty sac. The crosses on the scans are the markers that are used for making measurements.

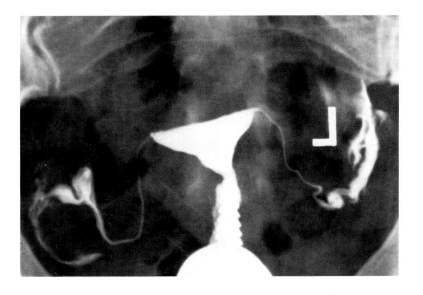

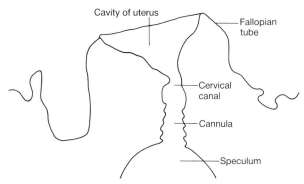

Cavity of uterus

Fallopian
tube

Cervical
canal

Cannula

Speculum

PLATE 3 (*a*). Normal hysterosalpingogram. A speculum is inserted into the vagina and dye that will show up on an X-ray is run via a cannula (metal tube) into the cervical canal and thence into the cavity of the uterus and along the Fallopian tubes.

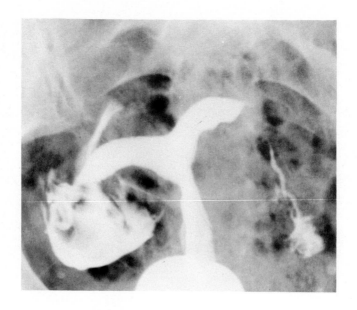

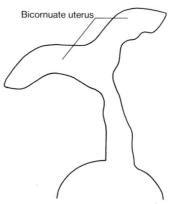

Bicornuate uterus

PLATE 3 (*b*). Hysterosalpingogram showing bicornuate uterus.

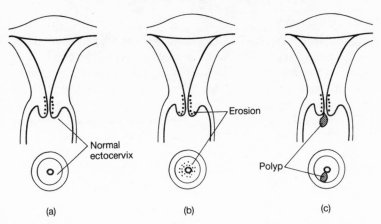

FIG. 4.3. (*a*) Normal cervix; (*b*) cervical erosion; (*c*) cervical polyp. The appearance of the cervix on speculum examination is shown in the lower part of the diagram.

The mucus-producing tissue is more fragile and bleeds more readily than the pink smooth tissue which usually covers the ecto-cervix. It is not uncommon for bleeding to occur after intercourse, or even spontaneously, when a cervical erosion is present. Provided that a cervical smear is normal a cervical erosion should be left untreated during pregnancy. It will often disappear in the weeks following delivery.

Cervical polyp

Another less common condition which may cause bleeding in early pregnancy is a cervical polyp (Fig. 4.3). This is a benign (non-malignant) spherical growth on a stalk that arises from the cervical canal. Polyps vary in size from a few millimetres to over a centimetre in diameter. They are covered in red mucus-producing tissue and may bleed spontaneously or when touched. They should be left alone during pregnancy and no attempt should be made to remove them as this may cause undue bleeding. They are usually found to have disappeared when the cervix is examined at the postnatal check up (approximately 6 weeks after delivery).

Cancer of the cervix

Although less than one in a thousand women who have bleeding in early pregnancy will be found to have cancer of the cervix, it is important that anyone with persistent vaginal bleeding should have a speculum examination so that the cervix can be looked at and a cervical smear can be taken.

Thus vaginal bleeding in early pregnancy is a common problem. In the majority of cases it will settle without treatment and the pregnancy will continue normally. In some cases, however, the bleeding will herald the onset of a miscarriage or it may be indicative of a different problem such as an ectopic pregnancy or a cervical abnormality.

5

Complete, incomplete, and missed abortion

The first warning that a pregnancy may end in a miscarriage is usually the occurrence of vaginal bleeding. In many cases, as discussed in the last chapter, vaginal bleeding in early pregnancy will cease and will not be followed by a miscarriage. Unfortunately, however, in some cases a miscarriage will take place. Usually the bleeding becomes heavier and painful uterine contractions commence. The pain is usually intermittent, coming every few minutes, as in labour. The amount of pain experienced differs from one woman to another, and in the same woman from one pregnancy to another, as does the time taken for a miscarriage to occur after the contractions have begun. This can vary from minutes to several hours. If the pain is severe a pain-killing injection can be given, provided that the possibility of an ectopic pregnancy has been excluded.

As the bleeding increases blood clots may be passed which resemble pieces of raw liver. The products of conception may also be expelled. These consist of placental tissue and membranes. Sometimes a recognizable fetus is present, but in early pregnancy, if the fetus has died some time before the miscarriage occurs, it may have dissolved away and no longer be identifiable. Any tissue that is passed should be saved for the doctor to look at. This examination is important for several reasons. Firstly, if recognizable placental tissue has been expelled a certain diagnosis of actual rather than threatened miscarriage can be made. Secondly, the presence of recognizable placental tissue will give proof that the woman was definitely pregnant. It is possible for there to be a delayed period followed by very heavy bleeding and the passage of blood clots without a woman being pregnant, and it can be very important in her future management to know whether or not she was pregnant. If, for example, this was a first pregnancy and the pregnancy is confirmed, and she had previously been concerned about infertility it will be clear to her and her doctors that there was no bar to conception in her case. Thirdly, examination of the products of conception may help to explain why the miscarriage occurred. Fourthly, it may be possible to tell whether the miscarriage is complete or incomplete.

Complete abortion

With a complete abortion all the products of conception are expelled from the uterus which is then empty so that there is no need for the woman to go into hospital for a curettage (scrape). The vaginal bleeding will become progressively less in amount and should cease after a few days. Very early miscarriages, before 7 weeks' gestation, are usually complete.

Incomplete abortion

Later miscarriages are, unfortunately, often incomplete and some pieces of placental tissue remain inside the uterus. This is a potentially dangerous situation as it is possible that heavy bleeding will occur and there is also a risk that the retained products of conception will become infected in due course. It is therefore important that medical aid should be sought if there is a possibility that the miscarriage is incomplete.

The reason why heavy bleeding may occur is that there is a very good blood supply to the uterus and placenta throughout pregnancy. With a miscarriage the placenta separates from the wall of the uterus and the maternal blood vessels are then exposed and are able to bleed. If the products of conception are expelled completely the muscle fibres in the wall of the uterus can contract and close off the exposed vessels. If, however, tissue is retained in the uterus the muscle fibres are unable to contract fully and heavy bleeding may ensue. Fortunately there are drugs available (such as ergometrine and syntocinon) which make the muscle fibres contract more efficiently, and the amount of bleeding can usually be temporarily reduced by the administration of one or both of these drugs. However, the only way to ensure that heavy bleeding does not recur is for the uterus to be emptied. This has to be done in hospital. Rarely, if bleeding has been very severe, it may be necessary to give a blood transfusion before or during the procedure or even, very occasionally, before the woman is transferred to hospital. If the woman is shocked owing to very heavy blood loss the doctor or ambulance crew can call the emergency obstetric flying squad who will resuscitate her with an intravenous infusion (drip), giving blood if necessary, before taking her to hospital.

As a general anaesthetic is usually required for evacuation of the uterus the woman should not eat or drink while awaiting transfer to hospital following a miscarriage. This is because it is important that a certain amount of time should elapse between eating or drinking and the administration of a general anaesthetic so that the stomach has time to empty, thus reducing the risk of vomiting and inhalation of the stomach contents into the lungs. If there is an urgent need to give an anaesthetic before this time elapses the anaesthetist will usually insert a cuffed endotracheal tube into the trachea (windpipe), after putting the woman to sleep, to reduce the risk of such inhalation occurring. The uterus is emptied with the aid of instruments. An injection of ergometrine or syntocinon is often given to encourage the uterus to contract and to reduce the blood loss. After the operation there should be no pain other than the discomfort, like a period pain, caused by a well-contracted uterus; the amount of bleeding will be similar to that which occurs during a normal period. The nurses will check the pulse and blood pressure and the blood loss for some hours after the procedure. Once they are satisfied that the woman's condition is stable and that she is properly 'round' from the anaesthetic and not nauseated she will be able to eat and drink, and to get up and about. If she is Rhesus negative she should receive an injection of anti-D to minimize the likelihood of her developing anti-Rhesus positive (D) antibodies.

Practices vary but she will usually stay in hospital for one night after the operation and then be able to go home the next day, provided that all is well and her temperature is not raised.

Sometimes the woman will find that her breasts will become uncomfortable and start leaking milk after a miscarriage. The later in pregnancy that the miscarriage occurs, the more likely this is to happen. Provided that the milk is not expressed (squeezed out) the breasts will usually stop leaking without any special treatment, but occasionally drug treatment will be needed.

It is normal for the woman to experience a deep sense of loss following a miscarriage—this is discussed further in Chapter 10.

Septic abortion

Fortunately infection does not usually occur following a spontaneous abortion if the uterus is emptied at the time of, or within a few hours of, the miscarriage. However, infection can arise at any time and if it does it is important that it is adequately treated as otherwise it may ascend from the uterus to the Fallopian tubes and cause salpingitis (inflammation of the Fallopian tubes). This can lead, in a small percentage of cases, to permanent damage of the Fallopian tubes and to subsequent infertility. Another danger is that occasionally the infection can spread beyond the Fallopian tubes into the abdominal (peritoneal) cavity causing peritonitis and a severe generalized illness.

Fortunately with modern antibiotics bacterial infection can usually be brought rapidly under control. It is essential, however, that an adequate course of the appropriate antibiotics is completed to ensure that the infection is completely eliminated.

Missed abortion

This term is used to describe the situation that can arise when a fetus dies but is not expelled. It is 'missed' in the sense that a miscarriage has not occurred, rather than that it has occurred without anyone noticing. Initially the woman will be unaware that anything is wrong but then she may notice that her pregnancy symptoms are subsiding and that she no longer feels pregnant. There may be some vaginal bleeding. If a vaginal examination is performed the uterus will usually be found to be smaller than the size expected for the known length of gestation.

Complete, incomplete, and missed abortion

The best method of confirming or refuting a diagnosis of missed abortion is to perform an ultrasound scan. If the fetus is alive the fetal heart can usually be seen to be beating after 8 weeks' gestation. By about 12 weeks' gestation it should be possible to hear the fetal heart sounds using a portable doppler ultrasound machine, which is a simpler piece of apparatus than an ultrasound scanner. Using it, the woman will be able to hear the fetal heart sounds too, if they are present, and this will obviously be very reassuring. In early pregnancy it will usually be necessary to perform more than one ultrasound scan before a diagnosis of missed abortion can be made with certainty. A pregnancy test is less helpful than an ultrasound scan because, as mentioned previously, it can remain positive for some days after the fetus has died.

It is obviously very distressing for a woman to know that she is carrying a fetus which is no longer alive, and for this reason most women will be anxious to have the uterus emptied once the diagnosis of missed abortion is certain. Such a course of action will also spare her some of the trauma of a spontaneous miscarriage. It is clearly extremely important, however, to be quite sure of the diagnosis before the uterus is emptied. The only medical danger in not evacuating the uterus promptly is that occasionally changes will occur in the blood, after a few weeks, which may make it clot less well. These can be tested for, and if necessary treatment with the appropriate clotting factors can be given.

Continued bleeding following a miscarriage

If heavy bleeding continues following a miscarriage, or following evacuation of retained products of conception, it is likely that some products are still present in the uterus and that curettage or recurettage is necessary.

Advice following a miscarriage

Because of the danger of introducing infection it is wise not to use tampons for the bleeding that occurs after a miscarriage and not to resume intercourse for at least 2 weeks. Many women will prefer to wait to have intercourse until after they have had a period. It is common for couples to find that their sex drive is reduced for a while after a miscarriage.

The normal cycle usually recommences soon after a miscarriage, and a period commonly occurs within 4-6 weeks. This is usually preceded by ovulation, and so if a couple wish to have intercourse and to avoid conception for a while some form of contraception should be used. If birth-control pills are the preferred method of contraception they can be started the day after the miscarriage occurred. Extra precautions (such as the sheath) should, as usual, be used during the first month after starting the pill.

It is generally advisable to wait 2 or 3 months before trying for another pregnancy, but there is no known risk attached to becoming pregnant straightaway. A delay of a few months allows for physical and emotional adjustment but is not essential. It used to be helpful to allow a regular cycle to resume before becoming pregnant so that the next pregnancy could be dated accurately, to allow optimum management, but with the advent of ultrasound scans this is no longer so important.

Outlook for the future

The likelihood of achieving a successful pregnancy following a miscarriage will obviously depend on the reason why the miscarriage occurred. However, in statistical terms, if a woman's first pregnancy ended in miscarriage she is probably only very slightly more at risk of a miscarriage in her second pregnancy than someone of the same age and background who has had no miscarriages. Following two consecutive miscarriages the chance of the next confirmed pregnancy ending in the birth of a live healthy baby is still about 70 per cent, and even after three miscarriages it is greater than 50 per cent. None the less, if a woman has three or more consecutive miscarriages it may be helpful to consider undertaking some special investigations (see Chapter 9). Advice on precautions to be taken in the next pregnancy is given in Chapter 11.

6

The incidence of spontaneous miscarriage

The true incidence of spontaneous miscarriage is very difficult to determine for a variety of reasons. If the term miscarriage is used to include the loss of a fertilized ovum at any stage of its development up to 28 weeks, it is clear that many 'miscarriages' will occur before a menstrual period has been missed and thus without the woman ever knowing that she had conceived. Complete abortions can also occur after a missed period without the woman realizing that she was pregnant. Even if she is aware that she was pregnant she may not be seen by a doctor and the miscarriage may not then be confirmed or recorded. Another problem that can arise is that a woman can miss a period and then have heavy bleeding and think that she is miscarrying, and yet she may not in fact have been pregnant. It may be difficult to prove whether she was pregnant or not.

Apart from these problems the incidence of spontaneous miscarriage is likely to vary between different groups of women—for example between those of different ages and different genetic and environmental backgrounds. None the less, by the undertaking of carefully planned surveys and by the measurement of pregnancy-specific hormone levels in women trying to conceive, knowledge about the true incidence of spontaneous miscarriage has increased. It is clear that the rate of loss is very high in early pregnancy and that in general it decreases as pregnancy progresses.

Miscarriages before pregnancy is confirmed

Pre-implantation loss
At the present time it is impossible to know how often an ovum is fertilized and fails to implant in the uterus, but it is likely that many fail to do so.

Post-implantation loss

After implantation the developing embryo produces increasing amounts of human chorionic gonadotrophin (HCG). Measurement of HCG forms the basis of the standard urinary pregnancy test which usually becomes positive by 2 weeks after a missed period. For this test HCG levels have to be relatively high, but for research purposes very sensitive assays have been developed which can detect low levels of HCG in the blood or urine, and which can demonstrate the presence of a pregnancy 7–14 days after fertilization. It has been estimated from recent studies using these and other techniques that between 10 and 30 per cent of fertilized ova are lost after implantation without the women concerned being aware that they were pregnant.

Miscarriages in confirmed pregnancies

It is somewhat easier to determine the number of pregnancies that are lost after a period has been missed and the woman knows that she is pregnant. It is thought that 10–20 per cent of such pregnancies are lost before 14 weeks' gestation (first trimester of pregnancy) and that a further 2–3 per cent are lost during the next 14 weeks (second trimester).

In many cases the fetus fails to develop normally. If embryonic development ceases at an early stage the amniotic sac may be empty—a condition sometimes referred to as a 'blighted ovum'. In such a case the situation is obviously hopeless. Once a fetal heart beat can be detected the risk of miscarriage is much reduced—to less than 5 per cent.

Thus most of the pregnancies that are lost are lost long before the fetus is capable of independent existence (Table 6.1). Fortunately in the majority of cases there is a very good chance that a subsequent pregnancy will be successful.

Risk of miscarriage in subfertile women

There seems to be a slightly greater risk of miscarriage in subfertile women than in women who have no difficulty in conceiving, both

TABLE 6.1
Approximate frequency of miscarriage at different times in pregnancy

	Approximate percentage of pregnancies lost through miscarriage
Post-fertilization, pre-implantation	Not known
Post-implantation to 4 weeks' gestation[a]	10–30
4–13 weeks' gestation	10–20
14–28 weeks' gestation	2–3

[a] 4 weeks' gestation means 4 weeks after the last menstrual period, i.e. 2 weeks after fertilization.

when they are not receiving any treatment and in some instances when they are receiving treatment. In either case the chance of a pregnancy being successful is still of the order of 70 per cent or more.

The incidence of miscarriage after *in vitro* ('test tube') fertilization is also currently higher than after natural fertilization, but it will probably decrease as techniques improve.

Multiple pregnancy (twins, triplets, etc.)

There is a somewhat higher risk of miscarriage in multiple pregnancies than when only one fetus is present. The risk of miscarriage is greater with identical twins than with non-identical twins, and also increases with the number of fetuses.

7

The causes of spontaneous miscarriage

Although knowledge about the causes of miscarriages has increased considerably in recent years there is still a great deal to be learnt. In most cases it will not be possible to be certain why a particular miscarriage occurred. Fortunately in most cases the next pregnancy will result in the birth of a healthy live baby irrespective of the cause of the miscarriage.

Causes of very early pregnancy loss—before a period is missed

Little is known about the causes of very early pregnancy loss because it has only recently been possible to diagnose pregnancy before a period has been missed by very sensitive measurements of hormone levels. It is likely that there are many causes of such pregnancy loss, and that these include some of the factors that have been found to be important in causing miscarriages after pregnancy has been confirmed.

Causes of miscarriage in confirmed pregnancies

It is convenient to divide miscarriages in confirmed pregnancies into first trimester (before 14 weeks' gestation) and second trimester (from 14 to 28 weeks' gestation) miscarriages. Miscarriages are much less common after 14 weeks' gestation, and it is more likely that a specific cause, other than a chromosomal abnormality, will be identified for a second trimester than for a first trimester miscarriage. There is, of course, some overlap between the causes of first and second trimester miscarriages. The more specific causes of second trimester (mid-pregnancy) miscarriages are discussed in the next chapter.

Causes of first trimester and some second trimester miscarriages

Chromosomal abnormalities

Fetal chromosomal abnormalities are the single most important cause of fetal loss in women. They are probably present in more than 1 in 20 confirmed pregnancies. In several large studies a fetal chromosomal abnormality was found in approximately 50 per cent of spontaneous abortions for which medical advice was sought, and in which a search for a chromosomal abnormality was made. Most chromosomal abnormalities are incompatible with survival and the great majority of fetuses with abnormal chromosomes are aborted spontaneously before the end of the first trimester.

Chromosomal abnormalities in a miscarriage can sometimes be detected by culturing the freshly expelled products of conception. After 1-4 weeks of growth the chromosomes of representative cells are examined. Success rates for culturing chromosomes in these circumstances vary from 60 to 90 per cent under optimum conditions.

Several different types of chromosomal abnormality occur—these arise at different phases of the life of the egg or sperm varying from the time that the mother or father were themselves fetuses to the time of the fusion of the egg and the sperm. Little is known about the cause of chromosomal abnormalities except in very rare cases where one of the parents has a rearrangement of their chromosomes whereby, for example, material from one chromosome is attached to another chromosome. Certain other factors such as increasing age of the mother are known to be associated with an increased risk of fetal chromosomal abnormality. Most fetal chromosomal abnormalities arise sporadically and do not recur in the next pregnancy. Culturing abortion material is difficult, expensive, and frequently unsuccessful. As it is often unrewarding it is seldom performed.

Other fetal abnormalities

It is likely that many miscarriages are due to severe fetal structural (e.g. heart or nervous system) abnormalities or biochemical disorders that are incompatible with life. These may be impossible to diagnose in early pregnancy even after a miscarriage has occurred, and the incidence of such abnormalities is therefore unknown.

Hydatidiform mole

A hydatidiform mole is an abnormal development of the placenta. It occurs in Britain and North America in about 1 in 2000 pregnancies, but is much more common in the Far East. The term hydatidiform refers to the fact that the abnormal placental (molar) tissue contains many small grape-like fluid-filled vesicles.

The first indication that something is wrong is usually the occurrence of vaginal bleeding. This may not start until the second trimester of pregnancy. The diagnosis is most frequently made by performing an ultrasound scan which shows a snow-storm appearance, and in most cases no fetus. Once the diagnosis is certain the uterus should be emptied, usually by suction aspiration under general anaesthesia. There is a small risk that some molar tissue may persist and increase in volume and occasionally develop into a rare form of cancer (choriocarcinoma) during the following months. Fortunately, persistent and malignant molar tissue can be detected by measuring human chorionic gonadotrophin (HCG) levels in the urine or blood, and effective treatment is available. Women are therefore asked to provide such samples for at least a year after they have had a hydatidiform mole and to make sure that they do not become pregnant during that time.

Increasing maternal age

Most studies have shown an increased risk of miscarriage in older women. This is partly accounted for by the known increased incidence of fetal chromosomal abnormalities with increasing maternal age, which has led to the offer of amniocentesis at 16 weeks' gestation, for the diagnosis of fetal chromosomal abnormality, to women in their forties and late thirties. At the age of 38 the incidence of chromosomal abnormality at 16 weeks' gestation is approximately 0.8 per cent, and at the age of 45 it is approximately 5 per cent. It is obviously higher earlier in pregnancy, as most chromosomally abnormal fetuses will be lost long before 16 weeks' gestation.

Other reasons for the increased risk of miscarriage in older women are less easy to evaluate. It is possible that some women conceiving late are relatively less fertile than other women, and that there is an association between their subfertility and their miscarriages.

Abnormality of the uterus

Many women with a uterine abnormality such as a congenitally abnormally shaped uterus or a fibroid uterus do not have any problems in pregnancy, but these abnormalities can occasionally cause miscarriages in both the first and second trimesters of pregnancy. They are discussed more fully in the next chapter.

Intrauterine contraceptive device

There is no increased risk of miscarriage in women who have used an intrauterine contraceptive device for contraception, provided that the device is removed before conception. If conception occurs with a device in place there is a significant risk of intrauterine infection and of miscarriage if the strings of the device are protruding through the cervix. These risks can be reduced by gentle removal of the device by a doctor in early pregnancy.

Maternal diseases

Diseases affecting the mother may occasionally cause miscarriages in either the first or second trimesters.

Infections. Most maternal infections do not cause any harm to the fetus but any really severe generalized infection, such as influenza or malaria, may lead to fetal death and miscarriage.

Some infectious agents which do not cause much maternal constitutional upset are known to cause an increased risk of fetal abnormality and of spontaneous abortion when they occur in early pregnancy. Steps are being taken to try to reduce the likelihood of these infections arising.

Rubella (German measles). It is well known that rubella infection in early pregnancy commonly causes severe fetal abnormality and even fetal death followed by spontaneous abortion. Considerable success in reducing the incidence of rubella in pregnancy has followed the widespread vaccination of children and of women who are not already immune to rubella. However, it is very important that vaccination programmes are maintained and that if possible a woman's immunity to rubella is checked *before* she tries to conceive so that she can be immunized at least 3 months before conception if she is found not to be already immune. Most women are checked routinely during pregnancy so that they can be offered immunization after delivery if they are not immune. Obviously, it is preferable that immunity should be checked before pregnancy when possible.

Syphilis. Syphilis is uncommon but if this infection is present in the mother it can have devastating effects on the fetus, causing either fetal death and late abortion or a variety of congenital abnormalities. Fortunately treatment of the mother with penicillin early in pregnancy is usually effective in preventing infection of the fetus. Although syphilis is uncommon it is tested for routinely in most pregnant women as intrauterine syphilis is so serious, if untreated, and is so easy to treat if it is diagnosed in time.

Other maternal diseases. Chronic maternal diseases rarely cause spontaneous abortion but there are some conditions in which the fetus is particularly at risk throughout pregnancy. These conditions include severe hypertension (raised blood pressure), severe renal (kidney) disease, diabetes, and some uncommon conditions such as phenylketonuria and systemic lupus erythematosus. Women with these conditions are likely to be already under medical care. They, and women with other medical disorders such as epilepsy, should talk to the doctor who is looking after them before embarking on a pregnancy so that the possible risks can be explained to them and their treatment can be modified if necessary.

Drugs

Drugs seldom cause abortion, but many drugs can cause fetal abnormalities if taken during early pregnancy. It is therefore very important that women should not take any drugs that are not essential in early pregnancy. This also means that they should not take such drugs when they are trying to conceive, as the pregnancy will have been present for at least 2 weeks before they have any suspicion that they may be pregnant. As mentioned above, women who are on medical treatment should discuss their treatment with their doctor before embarking on a pregnancy.

Operations in early pregnancy

Most types of surgery in early pregnancy do not increase the risk of miscarriage, but it is sensible to postpone any non-essential surgery at least until after the first trimester or preferably until after the baby is born.

Alcohol

There is good evidence that excessive maternal alcohol intake during pregnancy increases the risk of fetal abnormality. It is likely that the spontaneous abortion rate is also increased in women who drink excessively. The term fetal alcohol syndrome is used to include the severe fetal abnormalities that can occur in the babies of women who drink very heavily (the equivalent of about eight large glasses of wine a day). It is likely that there is a spectrum of abnormalities in women who drink less heavily and less frequently and it is not clear what a 'safe' level of alcohol intake is in early pregnancy. This may vary from one person to another, and clearly many women who drink the equivalent of one or two glasses of wine a day have completely normal babies. The best advice at the present time, however, must be either not to drink alcohol at all, or to drink very little both *before* conception and during early pregnancy.

Smoking

It has been found that the fetuses of women who smoke are likely to grow less well than those of women who do not smoke. Some studies have also shown an increased spontaneous abortion rate in women who smoke heavily. It is therefore sensible to stop smoking both *before* conception and during pregnancy.

Radiation

It is unlikely that any single diagnostic radiological investigation causes an increase in the incidence of fetal abnormality, or spontaneous abortion. However, in order to minimize the risk of exposing a developing embryo to radiation, most X-rays of the abdomen in women in the reproductive age group are performed only in the first 10 days of the menstrual cycle, and not at all during the first 3 months of pregnancy.

Diet

Diet before and during early pregnancy is obviously important, but it is not clear whether a poor diet is an important cause of spontaneous miscarriage in the western world at the present time. In the absence of adequate knowledge on this subject it seems sensible for women hoping to become pregnant to achieve a well-balanced diet both before conception and during pregnancy.

Immunological factors

These are discussed in Chapter 9.

Stress

It is possible that stress occasionally plays a part in causing a miscarriage to occur. This is certainly true in some animals, but it is not so easy to evaluate in women.

Paternal factors

These are obviously very important but they are even more difficult to assess than maternal factors. The quality of the semen can be influenced by illness and by drugs—including alcohol and nicotine—but examination of the semen is not helpful in determining the cause of miscarriages at the present time.

Environmental factors

Many studies have been performed to try to assess the influence of environmental factors on the spontaneous abortion rate in particular at-risk populations. These studies are difficult to perform well, and have usually been based on interviews and questionnaires which rely on recall of past events with no actual documentation of miscarriages. They require large numbers of at-risk and control women for any valid conclusions to be drawn.

The causes of spontaneous miscarriage

It is likely that some chemicals can cause an increased rate of miscarriage in women who are exposed to them in early pregnancy. It is also possible that the wives of men who work with certain chemicals may have an increased miscarriage rate, but so far few definite associations have been found. Several studies have, however, shown an increased risk of miscarriage in nurses and women anaesthetists working frequently with anaesthetic gases in early pregnancy. Clearly, further well-designed studies of such environmental hazards are very important.

8

Some specific causes of miscarriage in mid-pregnancy

Miscarriages unfortunately occur very commonly in the first 3 months of pregnancy, and when they do a specific cause is seldom found unless a fetal chromosomal abnormality is looked for. Miscarriages in the second 3 months of pregnancy are much less common, and when they do occur it is more likely that a specific cause will be found and that effective action may be able to be taken to reduce the likelihood of a further late (second trimester) miscarriage in a subsequent pregnancy.

Some of the causes of late miscarriage are shown in Table 8.1. Clearly many of the other factors mentioned in the previous chapter may also cause second trimester miscarriages.

TABLE 8.1
Some causes of late (second trimester) miscarriage

Structural abnormality of reproductive tract
Cervical abnormality—incompetent cervix
Uterine abnormality—congenital abnormality, uterine fibroids
Multiple pregnancy
Factors leading to fetal death in the second trimester
Chromosomal or other congenital abnormality
Placental separation
Rhesus disease
Maternal illness
Following diagnostic tests
Amniocentesis
Fetoscopy

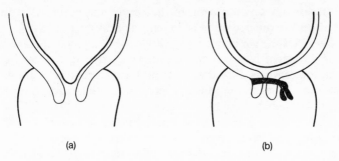

(a)   (b)

FIG. 8.1. (*a*) Membranes protruding through an incompetent cervix in mid-pregnancy; (*b*) incompetent cervix closed by cervical suture.

Incompetent cervix

This term is used to describe a condition in which the tissues of the cervix are unable to maintain closure of the internal os of the cervix during mid-pregnancy, so that a miscarriage inevitably occurs unless measures are taken to prevent it (Fig. 8.1). Cervical incompetence is probably responsible for more than 10 per cent of second trimester miscarriages. In most cases a fairly clear sequence of events precedes the miscarriage and the diagnosis can be made with reasonable certainty. In other instances, however, the diagnosis may not be so clear cut.

Cervical incompetence is not usually congenital, i.e. it is not usually a condition that is present from birth. Most often it is caused by instrumental dilatation of the cervix, or less frequently by other operations on the cervix such as a cone biopsy in which a cone-shaped piece of the cervix is removed. It is seldom caused by a routine 'dilatation and curettage' (D and C) as the cervix is not usually dilated very much during this operation. Most frequently it is caused by over stretching of the internal os of the cervix.

Some years ago some gynaecologists thought that severe dysmenorrhoea (painful periods) in adolescents could be relieved by forceful dilatation of the cervix with disruption of the cervical tissue round the internal os. It has been realized, however, that not only is this operation ineffective treatment for dysmenorrhoea,

45

but that it can actually damage the cervix and render it incompetent, and so the operation is no longer performed.

Nowadays the commonest surgical cause of an incompetent cervix is a vaginal termination of pregnancy during the course of which the cervix is dilated more than during a routine D and C to allow removal of the products of conception. The later the pregnancy is terminated the more the cervix has to be dilated. Gynaecologists are well aware of the possibility of damaging the cervix during termination of pregnancy operations and take great care to try to avoid causing such damage. The tissues of the cervix can also occasionally be damaged during a difficult delivery.

The typical sequence of events that occurs during pregnancy when the cervix is incompetent is as follows. The pregnancy usually proceeds normally until some time during the second trimester—most commonly between the 16th and 24th weeks of pregnancy. There may be an increase in the normal vaginal mucous discharge, and a feeling of heaviness in the vagina for a few days as the cervix shortens and begins to dilate. Then, often with very little warning and with few contractions, the cervix opens further and the pregnancy is expelled. The membranes may rupture first, allowing amniotic fluid to escape, or the sac may be expelled intact with the fetus inside it. The placenta may or may not be expelled. The fetus will be the appropriate size for the length of gestation and will usually be alive and completely normal but too immature to survive. If the placenta is not expelled soon after the fetus it may be necessary to remove it under anaesthesia.

The picture may be much less clear cut than this and it may be difficult to know whether or not a miscarriage was due to an incompetent cervix. It is very important to try to decide whether this was the cause, as if it was, late miscarriages will continue to occur in all subsequent pregnancies unless appropriate action is taken to prevent them. Fortunately effective treatment is available, but this will not prevent miscarriages due to other causes and it should only be used when it is likely that the cervix is incompetent.

Treatment of incompetent cervix

The aim of treatment is to support the internal os, and to prevent it dilating until the end of the third trimester. Several operations have been devised to achieve this aim. The ones most commonly performed consist of the insertion of a non-absorbable tape round the cervix at the level of the internal os (Fig. 8.1). This operation is often called 'insertion of Shirodkar (or McDonald) stitch or suture' after two of the doctors who have described such an operation. The stitch is usually put in at about the 14th week of pregnancy after the danger of a first trimester miscarriage (which is never due to an incompetent cervix) has passed and before the danger of a miscarriage due to an incompetent cervix arises.

Practices vary, but the woman is often admitted to hospital the day before the operation, which is normally performed under a general anaesthetic. She will usually be kept in hospital for a few days afterwards. She is then able to go home and resume her normal activities. She will usually be advised to refrain from sexual intercourse for about 2 weeks or occasionally longer.

The operation is simple and seldom causes any problems. Often there will be increased vaginal discharge during the pregnancy because of the presence of the suture material but usually no other side effects occur. The stitch is usually very effective if the right diagnosis was made. Occasionally, however, a miscarriage or premature labour may occur despite the insertion of a stitch and it is vitally important that the woman should report to hospital if she has any vaginal bleeding, leakage of fluid, or uterine contractions. If abortion or premature labour is occurring the stitch will have to be removed.

Ideally the stitch should remain in place until about the 38th week of pregnancy. It is then removed as it is no longer required and the chances of normal labour starting increase day by day. Removal is simple and does not usually require an anaesthetic. A speculum is inserted into the vagina; the stitch can be seen, and is easily held with forceps and cut with scissors and removed. The woman is then able to go home to await the normal onset of labour. A stitch will be required in all subsequent pregnancies.

Unfortunately the diagnosis of incompetent cervix is usually only made after a second trimester abortion has occurred, with loss of the pregnancy. Very occasionally the diagnosis is made in pregnancy before a miscarriage occurs if the cervix is found to be dilating. It may sometimes be possible to save such a pregnancy by inserting a stitch after the cervix has already begun to dilate.

There are no reliable tests that can be performed between pregnancies to make a certain diagnosis of incompetent cervix.

Abnormalities of the uterus

Abnormalities of the shape of the cavity of the uterus may be congenital (i.e. something that a person is born with) or due to the presence of fibroids in the wall of the uterus.

Congenital abnormalities of the uterus

These are fairly common—they are probably present in about one in a hundred women. Many different abnormalities can occur; they arise because of the way in which the uterus develops in a female fetus. It is formed by fusion of two hollow ducts. The walls of the ducts normally break down where they are in contact with one another to form the uterus, so that there is normally only one uterine cavity with a Fallopian tube on each side. Failure of development of one duct, or of fusion of the ducts, or failure of breakdown of the adjoining walls after fusion can occur, leading to a variety of uterine abnormalites, some of which are depicted in Fig. 8.2.

The diagnosis of a uterine abnormality is sometimes made on vaginal examination—if for example a double vagina or double cervix is present—but these particular abnormalities are uncommon and the diagnosis is more often made by performing an X-ray examination known as a hysterosalpingogram.

A hysterosalpingogram is an X-ray examination which is designed to give information about the cavity of the uterus and the state of the Fallopian tubes. It is usually performed in an X-ray department without an anaesthetic. It is important that it is performed in the follicular phase of the menstrual cycle, i.e. soon after the end of a period and before ovulation, so that there is no risk of irradiating a fertilized ovum or embryo.

Following a vaginal examination a speculum is introduced into the vagina, and the cervix is grasped gently to steady it. This may

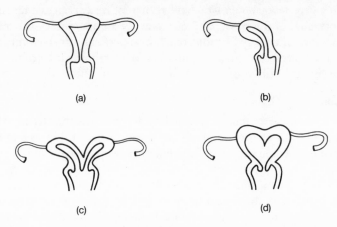

(a)

(b)

(c)

(d)

FIG. 8.2. Some congenital abnormalities of the uterus: (*a*) normal uterus; (*b*) unicornuate (one-horned) uterus; (*c*) bicornuate (two-horned) uterus; (*d*) uterus with septum.

be momentarily uncomfortable. A small tube is then introduced into the cervical canal so that dye which will show up on an X-ray can be injected into the cavity of the uterus and along the Fallopian tubes. At the same time as the dye is injected the abdomen is screened, using an X-ray machine, and the dye can be seen on a nearby television screen filling and outlining the cavity of the uterus and then flowing along the tubes. Two or three X-ray pictures are usually taken so that there is a permanent record of the findings (Plate 3). The instruments are then removed and the woman is able to go home after a short rest. Discomfort similar to a period pain may be experienced as the dye enters the uterus; it is usually short lived.

In many cases uterine abnormalities cause no problems during pregnancy but problems can occasionally arise. Rarely, a uterine abnormality such as a bicornuate uterus will cause recurrent miscarriages but more often a miscarriage in someone with a uterine abnormality is due to a cause other than the abnormality. In most cases the pregnancy will proceed normally. I have even delivered normal healthy twins from a woman with a completely bicornuate (two-horned) uterus—there was a baby in each uterine horn!

In a very few women who have recurrent miscarriages a uterine abnormality is the cause, and occasionally an operation to correct the abnormality may be indicated. This operation involves cutting into and therefore scarring the uterus and may thus cause problems, including infertility, of its own. It is not often indicated.

Fibroids

Fibroids are very common non-malignant tumours that arise in the muscular wall of the uterus. They are rare before the age of 20 years but become increasingly common as women grow older, and are present in at least one in five women by the age of 40 years. They can vary in number from one to more than a hundred, and in size from less than 1 cm to more than 25 cm in diameter. Most often, however, they are less than ten in number and less than 10 cm in diameter.

No one knows why they arise or how to prevent them occurring. They are slightly more common in women who have not been pregnant than in those who have, and they are known to occur more commonly in Negro women than in Caucasian women. However, they are found frequently in women of all races whether or not they have been pregnant.

They may be in the wall of the uterus (intramural) or they may protrude into either the uterine cavity (submucous fibroids and fibroid polyps) or the abdominal cavity (subserous fibroids) (Fig. 8.3). They may cause considerable enlargement of the body and cavity of the uterus. Subserous and intramural fibroids are usually diagnosed by abdominal or vaginal examination. Submucous fibroids and fibroid polyps can be demonstrated by performing a hysterosalpingogram.

Many women with fibroids become pregnant and have no problems due to the fibroids during pregnancy. Occasionally, however, fibroids may cause a problem early in pregnancy or later on. Possible early pregnancy problems that may arise with a fibroid polyp or submucous fibroid include failure of implantation and early or late miscarriage. Problems that can arise later on in pregnancy are outside the scope of this book. It is unusual for fibroids to be the cause of recurrent miscarriages, and it is likely that, if a woman

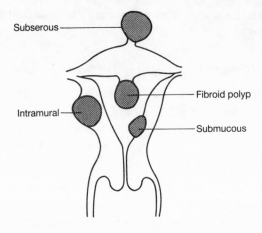

FIG. 8.3. Some possible sites for uterine fibroids.

with fibroids has one or even two miscarriages, they are caused by something other than the fibroids. However, if a woman is found to have a fibroid polyp it should certainly be removed. Removal of a submucous fibroid may or may not be indicated depending on whether it has caused problems or not.

Fibroid polyps can occasionally be removed vaginally, depending on their size and whether or not they have caused the cervix to dilate. An abdominal operation is required if the fibroid polyp is large and the cervix is closed, and is always required for the removal of submucous fibroids when their removal is indicated. The operation in which fibroids are removed and the uterus is conserved is called myomectomy.

In summary, fibroids are common but they seldom cause miscarriages unless they protrude into the uterine cavity. If they do protrude into the uterine cavity myomectomy may be indicated.

Multiple pregnancy

The risk of miscarriage in mid-pregnancy increases with an increasing number of fetuses. The risk is also higher in a twin pregnancy when the fetuses are identical (formed from one fertilized ovum) than when they are not identical (formed from two fertilized ova).

Factors leading to fetal death in the second trimester

Chromosomal or other congenital abnormality

Most severe chromosomal and other fetal abnormalities lead to miscarriage in the first trimester, but occasionally they will cause death of the fetus and miscarriage in the second trimester.

Placental separation

First trimester miscarriages usually start with vaginal bleeding and abdominal pain, caused by separation of some or all of the placenta from the wall of the uterus, before the pregnancy is expelled. Separation of the placenta before expulsion of the fetus is much less common in the second and third trimesters, but it may occur and it is then usually referred to as placental abruption. There may only be a small area of placental separation and the pregnancy may continue normally. On the other hand there may be sufficient separation of the placenta to cause fetal death, or to cause the uterus to contract and the cervix to dilate, with loss of the pregnancy.

If bleeding occurs during the second trimester of pregnancy the doctor should be contacted. If the fetus is alive the woman should rest in bed. Other causes of vaginal bleeding should be excluded. There is a good chance that the bleeding will settle and that the pregnancy will continue normally. If it is thought that some placental separation has occurred the pregnancy should be monitored more closely than usual to make sure that placental function remains adequate.

Rhesus incompatibility

This is an uncommon cause of fetal loss in the second trimester and has become even less common since the widespread administration of anti-D to women at risk of developing anti-Rhesus positive (D) antibodies.

Rhesus incompatibility arises when a Rhesus positive fetus is carried by a Rhesus negative mother who has developed anti-Rhesus positive antibodies. These antibodies can cross the placenta and cause breakdown of fetal red blood cells, thus causing fetal anaemia and sometimes fetal death in either the second or, more often, the third trimester. The antibodies usually develop in response to the leakage of some Rhesus positive fetal red cells into the mother's circulation at the time of a previous delivery or abortion. It has been found that the administration of anti-D to Rhesus negative women at risk, at the time of each delivery or abortion, greatly reduces the likelihood of the production of anti-Rhesus positive antibodies by the mother, and so Rhesus incompatibility is becoming much less common.

If a fetus is lost in the second trimester owing to Rhesus incompatibility the fetus will have died before the miscarriage occurs. The woman should be very carefully monitored during the next pregnancy by checking amniotic fluid samples taken by amniocentesis (see p. 16). If it is found that she is once again carrying a severely Rhesus affected baby intrauterine transfusion with Rhesus negative red cells may be indicated. A special needle containing a very fine plastic tube is passed, under local anaesthetic, through the mother's abdominal wall and through the wall of the uterus into the abdominal cavity of the fetus, using ultrasound to visualize the fetus. The needle is withdrawn and Rhesus negative red cells are then slowly transfused into the baby's abdominal cavity through the fine plastic tube.

Other blood group incompatibilities may also cause recurrent miscarriages.

Maternal illness
Some of the maternal illnesses which may adversely affect a fetus are discussed in Chapter 7.

Following diagnostic tests

Amniocentesis and fetoscopy
These tests are described in Chapter 3. The risk of miscarriage due to amniocentesis is approximately 0.5 per cent, and that due

to fetoscopy is approximately 3 per cent. The new technique of chorionic villus sampling, which is performed at about 9–10 weeks' gestation, should reduce the need for these tests to be performed when the present risk of miscarriage due to the procedure (up to 5 per cent) is decreased by improved techniques.

9

Recurrent miscarriages

Recurrent miscarriages can cause immeasurable unhappiness and despair to the couples who are unfortunate enough to experience them. All the emotions that may be engendered by a single miscarriage (as discussed in Chapter 10) are likely to be enhanced, and it becomes very difficult for the couple to believe that they will ever achieve a successful pregnancy. Fortunately, however, even after three consecutive miscarriages the next confirmed pregnancy has a better than 50 per cent chance of ending satisfactorily, without any treatment, with the birth of a live healthy baby. Even after four, five or more miscarriages the chance of a successful pregnancy is still greater than 40 per cent.

The underlying cause of each successive miscarriage is not necessarily the same. As chromosomal and other fetal abnormalities are so common in early pregnancy it is not uncommon for a woman to have a fetus with a chromosomal abnormality in one pregnancy and then a different problem in her next pregnancy, by chance.

For these reasons and because it is usually not possible to find a treatable cause for a miscarriage, there is seldom any point in a couple who have had less than three consecutive miscarriages having any investigations performed, or having any treatment, unless there appears to be a clear-cut reason for the miscarriages, such as an incompetent cervix, or there is some reason to believe that the woman has, for example, a relevant medical disorder. Even after three consecutive miscarriages it is unlikely that any specific abnormality will be detected and, as mentioned above, the chance of a successful pregnancy is still good. However, amongst couples who have three consecutive miscarriages there will be a few in whom a significant abnormality will be found, and it is therefore

55

TABLE 9.1
Some possible causes of recurrent miscarriages

Genetic factors	Rhesus incompatibility
Hormonal deficiency	Immunological factors
Cervical or uterine abnormality	Infections
Maternal medical disorder	

sensible to consider investigation after three consecutive miscarriages.

Possible causes of recurrent miscarriages

There is still considerable uncertainty about the importance of some of the factors listed in Table 9.1.

Genetic factors

Parental chromosomal rearrangement. As discussed in Chapter 7 it has been found that the fetal chromosomes are abnormal in at least 50 per cent of clinically recognizable miscarriages. Usually the next pregnancy will be chromosomally normal, but in a very few cases the abnormality is due to a parental chromosomal rearrangement and further fetal chromosomal abnormalities may occur. The risk of significant recurrent fetal chromosomal abnormality when one parent has a chromosomal rearrangement is variable. The couple should see a genetic counsellor for advice. In most cases there is a reasonable chance that a normal child will be conceived. If a pregnancy continues until 16 weeks' gestation fetal chromosome analysis can be performed on cells in the amniotic fluid, obtained by amniocentesis, to find out whether the fetus has normal or abnormal chromosomes. With the development of the new technique of chorionic villus sampling it is likely that fetal chromosome analysis will soon become a practical possibility in the first trimester.

The likelihood of finding a parental chromosomal abnormality in a couple who have had three consecutive miscarriages is less than 5 per cent.

Other genetic factors. It is known that some couples have an increased risk of conceiving a fetus which is abnormal despite having apparently normal chromosomes. Thus, if a couple have had one fetus with a neural tube (tissue from which the spinal cord and brain develop) defect such as spina bifida or anencephaly (a condition in which the brain fails to develop properly), they have a risk of approximately 1 in 20 of conceiving another fetus with a neural tube defect.

If it is found that recurrent miscarriages are due to a genetic problem on the father's side the possibility of artificial insemination of donor semen (AID) may be considered.

Hormonal deficiency

Progesterone is a hormone produced by the ovary and later by the placenta. It plays an important role in making the endometrium suitable for implantation and in maintaining pregnancy. It is possible that there is sometimes inadequate progesterone production in early pregnancy and that this could lead to early miscarriages, which could be recurrent. It is difficult to prove that this is the case but several studies have shown somewhat low levels of progesterone after ovulation in a few women with recurrent miscarriages.

Progesterone levels can be increased either by treatment with clomiphene during the early part of each menstrual cycle—this will cause the ovary to produce more progesterone after ovulation— or with progesterone suppositories. Successful pregnancies have occurred with both these forms of treatment. However, as mentioned earlier, even after three consecutive miscarriages there is at least a 50 per cent chance of successful pregnancy without treatment and so it is hard to be sure whether the good outcomes were due to the treatment or not. There have been no adequate trials of these forms of medication, and the possible risks of medication must be weighed up against the possible benefits in each particular case.

Cervical and uterine abnormalities

These are discussed in Chapter 8. The diagnosis of cervical incompetence is usually easily made from a knowledge of the history of the miscarriages—they usually occur after 14 weeks' gestation and are relatively rapid and pain free. There is usually a loss of mucus but no bleeding beforehand, and the fetus is normal and the appropriate size for the dates. Treatment is with a cervical suture in the next pregnancy.

Abnormalities of the uterus are a fairly uncommon cause of recurrent miscarriage, but after three miscarriages a hysterosalpingogram (see p. 48) may be performed so that the cavity of the uterus can be visualized. Abnormalities that may be detected include a congenitally abnormally shaped uterine cavity, submucous fibroids or fibroid polyps and, rarely, adhesions inside the uterus.

Maternal medical disorders

These are usually apparent in their own right and are discussed in Chapter 7.

Rhesus incompatibility

This is discussed in Chapter 8. Severe Rhesus and other blood group incompatibilities can very occasionally cause recurrent miscarriages. The fetus dies before the miscarriage occurs.

Immunological factors

The science of immunology has developed very rapidly in recent years and is continuing to do so. It is known that all human beings possess a very large number of cellular antigens (substances which provoke antibody formation) from an early stage of development. These antigens can stimulate an antibody response in other human beings if tissue is transplanted from one person to another, as in a kidney or heart transplant, and are responsible for the tissue rejection that may occur after such transplant operations.

The antigens are also very important in pregnancy—in a normal pregnancy the fetus will possess antigens from the father as well as the mother, and it might therefore be expected that the fetus would be rejected by the mother's body just as transplanted tissue is rejected if the immune system is not suppressed with drugs. The reason that not all fetuses are rejected is that immunological changes occur in a normal pregnancy that allow the mother's body not to reject the fetus. It is thought that it is in fact important that too many identical antigens should not be present in both the mother and the father, and that when they are the couple may have recurrent miscarriages as the appropriate immunological protective changes are not stimulated to occur.

Some women in whom such an immunological problem has been thought to be the cause of recurrent miscarriages have been successfully treated with injections of white blood cells during pregnancy. However, as discussed before, these successes might not have been due to the treatment. Controlled studies are now being performed to assess the value of this treatment in couples who have had several miscarriages and who are found to share several antigens, and to make sure that the treatment has no disadvantages.

Infections

Although an infection such as rubella (German measles) may cause a miscarriage if the mother develops it during early pregnancy, there is no definite evidence that infections other than untreated syphilis can cause recurrent miscarriages.

Possible investigations in a couple who have had recurrent miscarriages

It is very important that a full and clear history of all the woman's pregnancies and of her present and past health is obtained and that she is examined thoroughly before deciding which, if any, further investigations are appropriate. A detailed family history should also be obtained from both members of the couple, as this may reveal a genetic factor.

Investigations that may be recommended include chromosome analysis of both partners, blood grouping and testing for antibodies, hysterosalpingography, hormone estimations, and possibly immunological evaluation (Table 9.2). Chromosome analyses require special laboratory facilities but they do not cause much inconvenience to the couple as all that is required is a straightforward blood sample, as is also the case for checking the blood

TABLE 9.2
Possible investigations in a couple who have had recurrent miscarriages

In all cases
    Full medical, gynaecological, and obstetric history
    Family history
    General and vaginal examination

In appropriate cases
    Chromosome analysis of both parents
    Blood grouping and testing for antibodies
    Hysterosalpingogram
    Hormone estimations
    ? Immunological evaluation

group and testing for antibodies. The technique of hystero-salpingography has been described earlier (p. 48). Hormonal evaluation may entail measurement of progesterone levels in the second half of the menstrual cycle and in early pregnancy, and possibly the measurement of other hormone levels as well.

At the present time immunological evaluation is only undertaken in a few centres.

Treatment possibilities in couples with recurrent miscarriages

As mentioned at the beginning of the chapter a couple who have had three consecutive miscarriages for no obvious reason have at least a 50 per cent chance of a successful pregnancy without any treatment. This makes it very difficult to evaluate the efficacy of any particular therapy. It is very natural for couples to seek treatment and for doctors to wish to try to help with any treatment that might be of value, but this does not mean that giving treatment is necessarily the best course of action as most forms of treatment have some disadvantages.

General advice

Women who have experienced recurrent miscarriages are naturally very anxious and are usually keen to do anything that may help a pregnancy to succeed. It is obviously advisable for them to have a well-balanced diet and to avoid alcohol, smoking, and drugs at the time of conception and during early pregnancy in order to provide the optimum environment for the developing fetus.

Bed rest

Women who have had recurrent miscarriages for no known reason are usually advised to rest as much as possible during early pregnancy. Some women will find it reassuring to be admitted to hospital for rest, whereas others will prefer to stay at home. There is no definite evidence that rest increases the successful pregnancy rate, but it is quite possible that anything that helps to reduce anxiety may occasionally be beneficial.

Intercourse

The uterus contracts during orgasm and it is possible that this might increase the likelihood of miscarriage if the pregnancy is unstable. Many couples with recurrent miscarriages refrain from intercourse during early pregnancy in the hope that this will increase the chances of the pregnancy continuing. There is no definite evidence that this is in fact so, and it is probably equally important not to provoke marital disharmony. However, if bleeding has occurred it is probably wise to avoid intercourse for at least 2 weeks afterwards as this may be a sign that the pregnancy is already in jeopardy.

Specific treatment

If a specific cause for the recurrent miscarriages is found then the appropriate treatment should be given as described earlier.

Case history

The following case history may offer encouragement to women who have had several miscarriages and who find it hard to believe that they will ever have a baby.

A woman of 38 had had six pregnancies in 7 years and they had all ended in miscarriage—at 12, 6, 10, 6, 8, and 12 weeks' gestation respectively. No cause had been found for her recurrent miscarriages. She had had a normal hysterosalpingogram, and her chromosomes and her husband's chromosomes were normal.

She was admitted to hospital at 6 weeks' gestation in her seventh pregnancy for bed rest as she was naturally very anxious. Two days later she started to have slight vaginal bleeding. This continued intermittently during the next 6 weeks and was sometimes associated with lower abdominal pain and the passage of small clots. At 8 weeks' gestation an ultrasound scan showed that the fetus was alive and the right size for the dates. A further scan at 12 weeks' gestation showed that the fetus was alive and growing satisfactorily. She went home at 14 weeks' gestation. Her pregnancy was straightforward from then on, and she delivered a normal healthy baby boy weighing 7 lb at 38 weeks' gestation.

She became pregnant again 9 months later and was so busy with her baby that she was unable to take much extra rest during the pregnancy. She once again had some bleeding during the early weeks, but otherwise the pregnancy was straightforward. She delivered another normal healthy boy weighing 6 lb 8 oz at 38 weeks' gestation. No treatment other than rest was given in either pregnancy.

10

The emotional effects of miscarriage

A miscarriage is usually a deeply distressing event to the woman concerned and to those who are closest to her. She, her partner, and her closest relatives are likely to be the people most affected, but obviously circumstances will vary from one woman to another.

The couple will have experienced the joy of achieving a pregnancy and of anticipating the arrival of a baby. Even early in pregnancy the baby may feel very real to them and they may have an image of it in their minds, choose possible names for it, and make extensive plans for its future. As the pregnancy proceeds more relatives and friends will know about it, and more physical preparations for the arrival of the baby will be made such as decorating the nursery and purchasing equipment and even toys.

The later in pregnancy that the miscarriage occurs the greater the parents' distress is likely to be, but an early miscarriage can be equally traumatic, particularly if there was some degree of infertility or lack of awareness of how common early miscarriages are.

When a miscarriage occurs it may be very difficult for outsiders who have not experienced a similar loss to appreciate the enormity of what has happened to the couple and to understand that the fetus may have been a very real person to them, with an identity, and that the loss of the pregnancy may leave them grief stricken for a considerable period of time. Such lack of understanding may isolate the couple from their acquaintances and make their distress even greater than it need be. People may be afraid to talk to them about what has happened as they do not know what to say, and they may therefore shun them, as may happen with other types of bereavement. With better awareness of the feelings and problems

63

that the couple face some of their suffering can be alleviated. They need people to talk to who can listen and understand.

Emotional effects of miscarriage on the woman

Many emotions may be engendered by a miscarriage, and different ones will come to the surface at different times in the days and weeks following the miscarriage. These emotions include fear of the process of miscarriage and about the future, profound disappointment, grief, anger, self pity, feelings of inadequacy, failure, and helplessness, guilt, jealousy of those who have children, overwhelming sadness, and sometimes prolonged depression.

All these feelings may persist for a long time and are easily reawakened by a wide variety of stimuli—particularly by such events as casual contact with pregnant women and children when out shopping, careless remarks by relatives, friends, and acquaintances, photographs and articles in newspapers and magazines, and programmes on the radio or television—or they may just return out of the blue. It is particularly likely that they will be reawakened on the date when the baby was due and on anniversaries of that date, at times of family reunion such as Christmas, and also during a subsequent pregnancy.

The emotions that a woman feels and the strength of these emotions will obviously depend on her situation and her previous experiences. Some women will find it easier to cope than others, but most will be upset to a greater or lesser extent. The pregnancy may even have been unplanned and the woman may have had mixed feelings about it, or have been very upset by it, but even then it is common for her to feel guilty about the miscarriage. She may feel that the fact that she was not pleased about the pregnancy somehow caused the miscarriage to occur.

Much can be done to help by the people with whom the woman comes into contact at the time of the miscarriage and in the days and weeks afterwards.

Fear of the process of miscarriage and about the future
It is very important that the woman receives an appropriate and sympathetic explanation of what is happening at the time of the

miscarriage, and of what is likely to happen in the future, from the doctors and nurses who look after her. This will help to reduce her fear and her feelings of inadequacy and guilt, which may well be partly based on misapprehensions. Such help is not always forthcoming, but it can make a tremendous difference. Fortunately, medical and nursing staff are becoming more aware of the importance of spending time with women who are having and who have had miscarriages, and of encouraging them to express their fears and other emotions and to ask questions.

Disappointment and grief

The woman should be encouraged to express her feelings and to realize that it is normal for someone who has had a miscarriage to feel very strong and often uncontrollable emotions. If appropriate she must be encouraged to grieve for the lost pregnancy, the lost baby. If the pregnancy was fairly far advanced it may be helpful for her to see the fetus and to know what sex it is. It may help her to talk to someone who has been through the same experience as she has. For someone just to say 'don't worry, you can always try again' or 'better luck next time' is not appropriate.

Anger, self pity, and feelings of inadequacy, failure, and helplessness

At some stage the woman is likely to feel either anger or self pity, or both these emotions. She will say to herself: 'Why me?' If she has given up her career to start a family she may feel bitter and resentful.

She is also likely to experience feelings of inadequacy and helplessness and to wonder why she has failed to achieve what so many other women appear to achieve without any problems. This feeling of inadequacy may extend to other areas of her life, resulting in a general loss of confidence.

It may help her a little to realise that miscarriages are extremely common, and that many women who appear to have had no difficulties have in fact had a miscarriage at some stage. She should be aware that the fact that she has shown that she is fertile means that there is a very good chance that she will have a successful pregnancy in the future.

Feelings of guilt

It is normal for the woman to feel that she is in some way responsible for the miscarriage and to go over the events of the preceding days and weeks time and time again in her mind. 'If only . . . .' she will say to herself. She may worry that she ate or drank the wrong things, that she took too much exercise or went on too long a journey, that she had intercourse the night before, that she was too anxious, that she was not as happy about the pregnancy as she should have been, that she tripped and fell a few days before the miscarriage, that she is not worthy of being a mother, or about a whole host of other things. She may think that things would have happened differently if she had called the doctor earlier, or if she had seen a different doctor, or had been admitted to a different hospital.

It is very unlikely, however, that any action on her part, or on the part of her medical attendants, was in fact responsible for the miscarriage, and she must be encouraged to express her fears so that she can be appropriately reassured. Many women take some comfort from the fact that the fetus may well have been abnormal, and that it would have been even more distressing to have miscarried later in the pregnancy or to have had an abnormal baby.

Emotional effects on the woman's partner

The partner's initial concern is likely to be for the woman's health and safety. He may initially fear for her life if she is bleeding heavily and has to be admitted to hospital as an emergency. Later he may fear that there will be permanent damage to her (which is very unlikely) and that she may be infertile or that the problem will recur and that they may remain childless. Like her he may feel disappointed, angry, self-pitying, inadequate, helpless, guilty, and depressed.

It is likely that more sympathy and understanding from medical and nursing attendants, and relatives and friends, will be extended to the woman herself than to him, and he may feel resentful and left out. It is important, though, for him to feel that his grief is also recognized, even though he may feel that it is unmanly to express his emotions openly. He may try to hide his feelings of disappointment from his partner, thinking that she may become more depressed if she knows how disappointed he is, but if he does this she may think he is insensitive. By keeping his feelings bottled up he may become more depressed later on.

He may feel guilty that he was not more helpful with the daily chores during early pregnancy, or that he had to be away on business, or that there is something wrong with his genes. As in so many other situations good communication and full understanding of each other's feelings are of the utmost importance, and a couple who can share their feelings with each other will obviously be of enormous help and support to one another.

In many cases, perhaps fortunately, it will never be known whether the reason for the miscarriage was maternal or paternal, i.e. whether it was due to a fault in the ovum or the sperm, or some other factor. It is very important that neither the woman nor the man should feel guilty and blame themselves or each other unnecessarily for the miscarriage, and that their in-laws should not do so either. A great deal of distress can be caused by well-intentioned but uninformed comments from relatives and so-called friends. It is natural for people to look for explanations and reasons, but as mentioned earlier the cause of most miscarriages is seldom determined at the present time. Many are due to chromosomal abnormalities but we do not usually know the cause of these abnormalities.

Effects on children

If there are children in the household it is very likely that they too will be affected by the miscarriage. Even if they have not been told of the pregnancy they will know that something is wrong, and they will be upset by their parents' obvious or concealed grief. They may feel left out and neglected unless they are allowed to share in their parents' experience. They too may feel guilty and feel that the miscarriage was somehow their fault—if for example they knew that their mother was pregnant and they had been scolded for making her tired or for upsetting her, or for jumping on her, or if they resented the thought of an addition to the family. It should be explained to them, in terms appropriate to their understanding, that the miscarriage was nobody's fault.

Thus a miscarriage can have many deleterious psychological effects on a family, but much can be done to minimize any serious long-term consequences by careful and sympathetic understanding, explanation, and reassurance. With appropriate help most couples will find the strength to cope with the situation.

Pregnancy after miscarriage

The majority of women who have one, two, or even three or more miscarriages will also have successful pregnancies. They may find this hard to believe, especially after several miscarriages, but it is true.

For most women the chance of having a successful pregnancy after a pregnancy that has ended in miscarriage is very good. After one or two miscarriages the probability of the next confirmed pregnancy ending with the birth of a live healthy baby is almost the same as if there had never been a miscarriage. After three consecutive miscarriages the chance of the next confirmed pregnancy being successful is still greater than 50 per cent, and even after more than three miscarriages the chance of a successful pregnancy is still greater than 40 per cent.

When to try again

The best time to start trying again will vary from one couple to another. It is generally advisable to wait about 3 months to allow physical, and more particularly, emotional adjustment to occur. Some couples will need more time than this to mourn the loss of the pregnancy adequately, and should they start a new pregnancy before they have had time to work through their grief, they may experience a prolonged resumption of grief during the next pregnancy and after the birth of their new baby, and they may find it difficult to relate to the new baby.

Special precautions before conception

It is obviously sensible to try to achieve the best possible environment for the developing fetus. If the woman is not already immune to rubella it is advisable for immunization to be performed soon after the miscarriage, so that 3 months can elapse before she wants to try to become pregnant again. Adequate contraceptive precautions should be taken for 3 months after rubella immunization.

The woman should have a well-balanced diet, and smoking and alcohol intake should be stopped or reduced to a minimum. No drugs that are not essential should be taken. If the woman has a medical disorder she should discuss the management of this with her doctor before conception occurs, so that adjustments to her treatment can be made if necessary.

Unnecessary stress should be avoided. It is natural for the woman to be very anxious, but her anxiety can be reduced if she has plenty of support and understanding from those closest to her and by sympathetic reassurance from her doctor. It is important that she should have confidence in her medical attendants.

In most cases the cause of the previous miscarriage will not be known, or even if it is known, no specific treatment will be available or required, but the above precautions should help to increase the likelihood of a successful pregnancy.

Advice during early pregnancy

It may be wise not to tell too many people about the pregnancy too soon in case another miscarriage does occur, even though this is statistically unlikely. It can be more upsetting if too many people know about it. On the other hand, telling close friends about the pregnancy will bring understanding and support from them whatever the outcome is.

Some women feel superstitious about admitting that they are pregnant in case this brings bad luck. Others will feel that the pregnancy is unreal anyhow and will not be able to believe that they can carry a pregnancy successfully. They may not make any preparations for the care of the baby until late in pregnancy or even until after the birth of the baby. They should, however, be encouraged to make preparations, at least during the third trimester, as otherwise they may feel that the baby is unreal when it is born, and they may find it difficult to relate to the baby and to believe that it will live.

A woman who has had a miscarriage in a previous pregnancy is likely to be very anxious, to be very easily upset emotionally, and to think a lot about her previous miscarriage. She may have nightmares about having another miscarriage. Such anxieties and emotional lability are normal, and her partner and friends should be aware of this and give her plenty of sympathy, encouragement, and support.

Sexual intercourse

It is very unlikely that sexual intercourse will harm the pregnancy, but some couples will prefer to refrain from intercourse in early pregnancy when they have had a previous miscarriage.

Bleeding in early pregnancy

It is important to remember that many women experience bleeding in early pregnancy and do not miscarry. Once a fetal heart beat has been detected the chance of the pregnancy being successful is greater than 90 per cent, even when there has been some bleeding.

Specific treatment

Only very rarely does any specific treatment improve the outlook for the pregnancy. One instance where treatment is essential is if the woman has an incompetent cervix. In this instance mid-pregnancy miscarriage will inevitably occur if she does not have a cervical suture inserted (see p. 46).

In the majority of cases there is no specific treatment that will reduce the likelihood of a miscarriage occurring, but the chances of a successful pregnancy are usually good, even after three miscarriages, without any specific treatment.

Glossary

Technical words have usually been defined in the text where they first occur. They can be traced by using the index. Some of them are also defined here for easy reference.

Abortion (miscarriage): The loss of a pregnancy from the uterus before 28 weeks' gestation (see Chapter 1).

Alpha fetoprotein (AFP): A fetal protein normally found in very small amounts in the mother's blood. The mother's blood level of AFP is raised in certain circumstances, such as fetal spina bifida (see p. 15).

Amniocentesis: A procedure in which a fine needle is introduced through the mother's abdominal wall into the amniotic sac in order to obtain a sample of amniotic fluid for analysis (see p. 16).

Amniotic fluid: The fluid surrounding the fetus.

Amniotic sac: The sac, formed by the amnion and chorion (membranes), in which the fetus lies inside the uterus.

Antibodies: Substances produced by the body to protect it against infection and other foreign materials (antigens).

Anti-D: Anti-Rhesus positive (D) antibodies that can destroy Rhesus positive red blood cells (see p. 52).

Antigen: A substance which provokes antibody formation by the body.

Blighted ovum: A pregnancy in which the embryo ceases to develop very early on. The amniotic sac may only contain fluid and no tissue when the miscarriage occurs.

Blood groups: The main blood groups which are tested for in pregnancy are the ABO and Rhesus blood groups. Everyone has either A, B, O, or AB blood and is either Rhesus positive or Rhesus negative.

Cervical canal: The passage through the cervix connecting the body of the uterus and the vagina.

Cervix: The neck of the womb (uterus) (see Fig. 2.1).

Chorionic villi: Microscopic finger-like processes which form the main substance of the placenta (afterbirth).

73

Glossary

Chromosomes: Structures, each consisting of two connected rods which are made up of thousands of genes, which transmit all the hereditary information necessary for the development and formation of the tissues of the body. Every human cell (other than the ova and sperms) normally contains 23 pairs of chromosomes (see Plate 1).

Complete abortion: All the products of conception are expelled from the uterus and a curettage is not necessary.

Cone biopsy: An operation in which a cone-shaped piece of cervical tissue is removed. It is sometimes performed when a cervical smear shows abnormal cells.

Congenital: Present at birth.

Corpus luteum: 'Yellow body'. A structure formed in the ovary from an ovarian follicle from which ovulation has occurred.

Dilatation and curettage (D and C): A minor operation in which the inside of the uterus is cleaned out (a scrape).

Ectopic pregnancy: A pregnancy growing outside the uterus, usually in one of the Fallopian tubes (see p. 23).

Embryo: The developing baby in early pregnancy.

Endometrium: The lining of the uterus.

Fallopian tubes: The tubes that form a passage from the ovaries to the uterus.

Fertilization: The fusion of an ovum (egg) and a sperm.

Fetoscopy: A specialized test in which a fine lighted telescope is inserted into the amniotic sac so that the fetus or fetal blood vessels can be visualized (see p. 17).

Fetus: The baby while still in the uterus.

Fibroids: Common non-malignant tumours that arise in the muscular wall of the uterus.

Follicle: An ovarian follicle consists of an ovum and the layers of cells that surround it.

Follicle-stimulating hormone (FSH): A hormone secreted by the pituitary gland which initiates the development of one or more ovarian follicles.

Follicular phase: The part of the menstrual cycle which precedes ovulation.

Genes: The minute units of which the chromosomes are made up. They carry all the hereditary information necessary for the development and function of the tissues of the body.

Genetic counsellor: A doctor who is qualified to discuss with couples who are, or who may be, at extra risk of having a child with an inherited disorder what the risk is and what the consequences might be, and whether there are any tests that could be done in pregnancy to show whether the fetus has or has not got the disorder.

Hormone: A chemical messenger that is made in one part of the body and affects the functions of cells in various parts of the body.

Human chorionic gonadotrophin (HCG): A hormone produced by the placenta. Detection of this hormone forms the basis of the standard pregnancy test.

Hydatidiform mole: An abnormal development of the placenta (see p. 38).

Hysterosalpingogram: An X-ray examination in which the inside of the uterus and the Fallopian tubes can be seen (see p. 48).

Incomplete abortion: Only some of the products of conception have been expelled and some remain in the uterus.

Induced abortion: Abortion that is caused intentionally.

Intrauterine transfusion: A procedure in which compatible blood is given to the fetus, usually via a very fine plastic tube inserted through the mother's abdominal wall and the uterus into the fetal abdominal cavity (see p. 53).

Laparoscopy: An operation in which a lighted telescope is introduced into the abdominal cavity so that the ovaries, tubes, and uterus can be seen.

Luteinizing hormone (LH): A hormone secreted by the pituitary gland. The increased release of this hormone on about day 13 of a normal menstrual cycle causes ovulation to occur approximately 24 hours later.

Membranes: The two layers of tissue forming the wall of the amniotic sac. The inner one is called the amnion and the outer one the chorion.

Miscarriage (abortion): The loss of a pregnancy from the uterus before 28 weeks' gestation.

Missed abortion: The fetus has died but a miscarriage has not yet occurred.

Mucus: A sticky substance produced by certain tissues, e.g. the glands in the cervical canal.

Glossary

Myomectomy: An operation in which fibroids are removed and the uterus is conserved.

Neural tube: The tissue from which the spinal cord and brain develop in the embryo.

Oestrogens: One of the two types of female hormones produced by the ovary and placenta. The other female hormone is progesterone.

Ovum: An egg (female reproductive cell).

Pituitary gland: A small (about 1 cm diameter) but very important structure lying in the middle of the skull under the lower surface of the brain. It exerts control over several other glands by the production of hormones (see p. 5).

Placenta (afterbirth): The structure attaching the fetus to the wall of the uterus, through which it obtains its requirements and through which its excretory products are transferred to the mother. The placenta also makes several hormones.

Pregnancy test: A test for pregnancy based on the detection of human chorionic gonadotrophin in the urine.

Products of conception: The fetus, placenta, and amniotic sac.

Progestogen: Progesterone and progesterone-like drugs.

Progesterone: A hormone which is produced in increasing quantities by the ovary after ovulation and by the placenta during pregnancy.

Rhesus antibodies: Antibodies produced by a Rhesus negative person in response to the presence of Rhesus positive red blood cells in his/her body (see p. 52).

Rubella: German measles. A virus disease which may cause severe fetal abnormalities if contracted in early pregnancy.

Salpingitis: Inflammation of the Fallopian tubes.

Septic abortion: An abortion accompanied by infection of the cavity of the uterus.

Speculum: An instrument which, when inserted into the vagina, allows the vaginal walls and cervix to be seen.

Sperm: A male reproductive cell.

Spina bifida: A condition in which some of the bony elements of the spine fail to join, leaving part of the spinal cord and its coverings exposed.

Suction aspiration: A method of emptying the uterus via the cervix.

Glossary

Threatened abortion: The occurrence of vaginal bleeding during the first 28 weeks of pregnancy.

Trimester: Pregnancy is divided into three trimesters. The first ends at 14 weeks' gestation, the second ends at 28 weeks' gestation, and the third ends with delivery.

Ultrasound: High frequency sound waves which can be used to visualize the fetus, the placenta, the amniotic fluid, and many other structures.

Uterus: Womb (see p. 4).

Weeks of pregnancy/gestation: The number of weeks since the first day of the woman's last menstrual period, assuming that she has an approximately 28 day menstrual cycle.

Womb: Uterus (see p. 4).

Index